AMERICAN IMPERIALISM
Viewpoints of United States
Foreign Policy, 1898-1941

THE ORIENTAL POLICY
OF THE UNITED STATES

Henry Chung

ARNO PRESS & THE NEW YORK TIMES
New York ★ 1970

Collection Created and Selected
by
CHARLES GREGG OF GREGG PRESS

Reprinted from a copy in The Hoover Institution Library

Library of Congress Catalog Card Number: 70-111737
ISBN 0-405-02008-2

ISBN for complete set: 0-405-02000-7

Reprint Edition 1970 by Arno Press Inc.
Manufactured in the United States of America

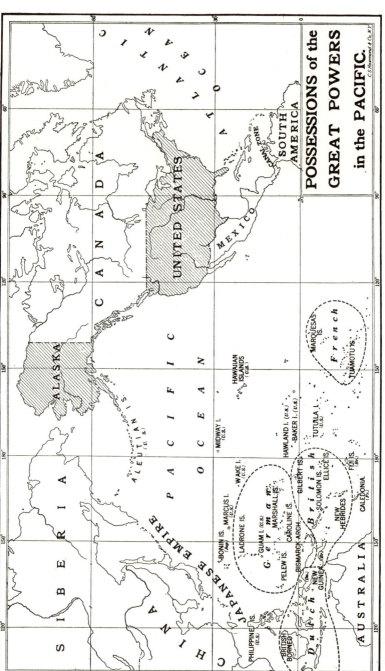

C.S.Hammond & Co.,N.Y.

POSSESSIONS of the
GREAT POWERS
in the PACIFIC.

Map showing, with those of other Powers, the American possessions in the Pacific. The United States has the longest coast-line of any nation on the Pacific; for its protection the American Navy in these waters should be second to none. Islands formerly under German control, held by the Japanese and British during the war, have been assigned, according to the terms of the Peace Treaty, to the mandatory of the Allied nations as follows: "The German Samoan Island—The mandate shall be held by New Zealand. The other German Pacific possessions south of the Equator, excluding the German Samoan Island and Nauru—the mandate shall be held by Australia. Nauru (Pleasant Island)—the mandate shall be given to the British Empire. The German Pacific Islands north of the Equator—the mandate shall be held by Japan." The German Colonies in the Pacific Ocean north of the Equator are the Ladrones, Caroline Marshall, and Pelew Islands.

The Oriental Policy of the United States

By
HENRY CHUNG, A. M.
*Compiler of Korean Treaties, Korean Envoy
to the Paris Conference*

With Introductory Note by
JEREMIAH W. JENKS, Ph. D., LL.D.
*Director of Far Eastern Bureau
Research Professor of Government and Public Admin-
istration ; New York University*

NEW YORK   CHICAGO
Fleming   H.   Revell   Company
LONDON   AND   EDINBURGH

To

The Chinese Students in America

*whose mission it is to emancipate their country
from the iron-bound traditions of the past and
to instil the spirit of Western civilization into
their ancient culture, so that China henceforth
will be not a passive and self-contained nation
but a progressive and dynamic power taking
its place, along with the United States, in the
family of the world's democracies*

Introductory Note

By

JEREMIAH W. JENKS, Ph.D., LL. D.

THE publication of a book on the Oriental policy of the United States is peculiarly timely.

In connection with the discussion and approval of the Treaty of Peace with Germany, and in connection with the much discussed League of Nations, it is essential that the government of the United States now determine its Oriental policy. It seems probable that the former policy of the territorial integrity of China and the Open Door, with fair dealing and justice, should be stated anew with a more vigorous determination to give it positive effect. If the policy is to be modified, the change should be made promptly and the world should know it.

It is fortunate that this book is written by a citizen of the Far East, a Korean. The people of the United States need to see clearly the view-point of the Orientals. There is little difficulty in getting the view-point of the Japanese. In fact, it is impossible for any reader of the public press to avoid getting the Japanese Government's view-point. It is much more difficult to know what the Chinese are thinking because of the great variety of opinions published in the press. Even the policy of the government of China is varying and undetermined, although the sentiments of the Chinese people now seem to be crystallizing. On the other hand, it has been almost impossible, owing to the Japanese censorship, to get an authoritative judgment or statement regarding Korean opinion.

This book is admirably written, and although I should not find it possible to agree in all particulars with the policies advocated and the views expressed, I believe it of very great importance to the American people that this view be known and understood in America.

The book, aside from expressions of opinions, contains very valuable information. Public men in the United States will find the documents published in the appendices of decided interest. They have not been heretofore readily accessible, but they are important.

It is especially desirable at this moment to be informed as fully as possible regarding the relations of Korea and Japan at the time when the Japanese Government is asking to have its influence over scores of millions of the people in China extended and strengthened. The whole civilization of the Orient, as well as the relations commercial, political and social, between the Orient and the West are swinging in the balance.

The public opinion of America and of Europe are determining factors. Everything that can throw real light upon the situation is valuable.

This book contains much of importance. It should be widely read.

J. W. J.

Preface

THE world's greatest war has come to an end, and, in so far as we are able to judge, autocracy and militarism have been driven from Europe once for all.

Now the all-important question is: "Is this the last war, or has the Peace Conference failed to solve the problem, thereby sowing seeds for another world war—perhaps more horrible than the one just concluded?"

Political cynics all over the world are already beginning to criticize the work of the Peace Conference as being no better than that of the Congress of Vienna; they assert that all the statesmen of the leading Powers went to the Peace Conference with the intention of getting out of it as much of material gain for their respective countries as they could, and that they have obtained as much as they had expected although not as much as they wanted; that the "Fourteen Points" were made a political revolving door to admit whatever the Powers wanted to have included, and to exclude nearly everything that did not serve their purposes of nationalistic gain; and that "self-determination" of weaker nations turned out to be selfish

determination of stronger Powers. These are
extreme views, unpleasant to be reminded of,
but, perhaps, they are not without foundation.

The League of Nations is as yet nothing more
than a mere experiment, basing its strength
upon the moral support of humanity. Will it be
a new Holy Alliance, or will it serve as the
framework for a world organization that will
bind humanity into a mosaic of lasting peace
and mutual good-will? The Peace Conference
has virtually recognized the validity of secret
treaties made prior to and during the war. Will
the Powers, under the guidance of the League
of Nations, abandon secret diplomacy and dis-
continue their economic exploitation of less civilized lands, thereby surrendering the particular
purpose of individual states to the common will
of mankind? Since the League of Nations is a
league of *free* nations, will it not, even if it becomes a complete success, be but another nail
driven into the coffin of the already crushed
nations, whose claims to the right of resurrec-
tion were denied them at the Peace Table? It
must be remembered that a right to revolt
against foreign oppression is an inalienable
right—a right upon the foundations of which
the Fathers of the American Revolution built
their nation. Peace at any price—especially, at
the price of the political aspirations of nations
whose people are crying for justice and free-

dom—is the worst kind of tyranny. It is, however, quite possible in this pregnant century,
that a new international standard of moral rec-
titude will be born of mankind, which will bring
pressure to bear upon the League so that this
new world organization will slowly succeed in
disentangling itself from the many things that
have bound us in the past, and be guided in its
actions by a sense of justice that plays no
favourites.

These are more or less academic speculations
that occupy the minds of political students at
the present as the aftermath of the war and the
peace settlements. But the most vital question
that is bound to engage the attention of the
statesmen of the world is the Far Eastern question.

The open door in the Far East cannot be
maintained permanently by a balance of rival
powers under the guidance of intrigue. China
must not be left to herself, staggering under the
strain of " spheres of influence," as she has been
during the last twenty years. The present
Eastern question is far more menacing to the
future peace of the world than was the Balkan
problem ten years ago. And if the Powers of
the world do not solve it now by peaceful
methods, then they must be prepared to solve it
ten years hence on the field of battle. It must
be remembered that China has one-fourth of

the world's population and an unlimited supply of natural resources—especially in coal and iron —to be exploited for peace or war. If this reservoir of power is permitted to be dominated by one nation—especially by such an ambitious empire as Japan—then it is obvious that the world cannot be made " safe for democracy "; there will be a drawn dagger at the heart of the United States and of the British possessions in the Far East. *Consolidation of Asia under Japanese domination* is the vision of the Japanese statesmen; and toward the attainment of this national goal there is unity of purpose among Japanese leaders. With this in view, Korea was annexed, Manchuria was absorbed, Inner Mongolia and Fukien province are being overwhelmed, and last but not least, Japan has obtained from the Powers at the Peace Conference the official recognition of her paramount interests in Shantung. At the present rate of Japanese aggression, China cannot last very long. Shall she be left to her own fate, or will the Powers of the West take an active interest in the Far Eastern affairs and save her national entity? The United States is not interested in any particular European or Asiatic problem, individual in character. But the United States *is* interested in a problem that has far-reaching effects on the world's peace and the welfare of mankind. What are her obligations, by treaty, by policy, by moral rights, to her sister Republic in the East? These are some of the questions the author has in mind in presenting the following chapters.

The author is not unaware of the possible criticism on the part of the reader that Parts I and II lack coördination. But the opinion of the writers on the Far Eastern questions are so often conflicting, even diametrically opposed to each other at times between those who regard the Japanese as a " model people " and those who regard them as "treacherous savages" masquerading in the garb of civilization, that it is almost impossible for the average American reader to have a clear-cut conception as to what the Oriental policy of the United States ought to be unless he knows the subtle undercurrent that directs, in a large measure, the course of public opinion in the West with regard to Japan's foreign policy. In this respect the author feels justified in considering the two parts as supplementary to each other.

In preparing this volume, the author had at his disposal abundant Oriental sources. But he took pains to use as much as possible only those facts that had been corroborated by Western historians and publicists of unquestioned integrity, in order that the reader may have available references for the fuller support of the present author's statements.

In conclusion, the author wishes to express his sincere appreciation of the kind encouragement and constructive criticism given him by Professor Hartley Burr Alexander, who has aided him to a deeper insight into and higher appreciation of Western culture.

New York.   HENRY CHUNG.

Contents

PART I

The Development of the Policy

15

PART II

*An Undercurrent Shaping the Policy:
Japan's Control of Publicity*

PART III

Documents in the Case

Maps

PART I

The Development of the Policy

Introduction

SOME years ago Ex-Premier Kang Yu-
Wei in an address before a group of
Chinese in California made a statement
that if China had been a strong and aggressive
empire, California would be to-day a part of
Chinese territory.[1] If we reflect for a moment
that at the time of the American occupation of
the Pacific coast, China was nearer to it than
any other great empire excepting Japan, and
that travel between China and California was
less difficult, before the time of railroads, than
that across the continent, we shall see that this
utterance from the wise Chinese is not an empty
remark. As early as 1860 there were 34,933
Chinese in the United States.[2] And it would
have been a comparatively easy matter for

[1] Kang was premier under the late Emperor Kwang-Hsu, and was
the leader of the reform movement of 1898. He has been the head
of Pao Huang Hwei (empire reform association), and is known
among the Chinese as the "Modern Sage." He made a trip around
the world in 1905-06 at which time the writer heard him in California.

[2] "Thirteenth Census of U. S., Abstract" (1910), p. 79.

China, had she been a powerful nation, to send colonies to the Pacific coast before that part of the continent became a part of the United States.[3]

It is also easy to believe that had the American Government, impelled by imperial tendencies, encouraged its merchants and seamen by subsidy and ample protection, the American "sphere of influence" would be to-day larger than that of any other nation in China, and American merchants would be enjoying the lion's share of the Oriental trade. The enterprising Yankees who sailed to all parts of the globe as merchants and fishermen were not at all slow in getting their share of the Oriental trade. Thus the first American merchant vessel appeared in Chinese waters in 1784;[4] and the commerce of the United States in the palmy days of its Oriental trade was second in volume among that of the Western nations. But American statesmen of the early period believed that there was "room enough for our descendants to the thousandth and thousandth generation" on this

[3] In 1850 California had a population of 92,597 (most of whom went out there after gold was discovered in 1848); Oregon had only 13,294; and the territory of Washington was not yet set off from Oregon, which act came on March 2, 1853.

[4] For a full account, see Callahan, "American Relations in the Pacific and the Far East," Johns Hopkins University Studies, XIX: 13 ff.; also, Coolidge, "The United States as a World Power," 313 ff.

continent,[5] and the American Government was too busily occupied with internal problems to safeguard the commercial interests of its citizens in the Far East. The intercourse, therefore, between North America and the Orient, built up at the close of the eighteenth century, was practically abandoned in later years, and so remained until the new efforts of the middle of the nineteenth century.

The industrial revolution of the nineteenth century inaugurated indeed a new political régime in Europe and in America. By utilization of steam, electricity, and labour-saving machinery, an industrial nation can produce manufactured articles far beyond its own needs. Two things are essential to commercial expansion of a nation—to find raw material either at home or abroad, and to find a market for manufactured goods. Commerce has become the greatest of all political interests. Territories are sought to enlarge commerce, and great armies and navies are maintained to enforce commercial rights in foreign lands. The United States, which had remained hitherto a self-contained nation, could no longer hold its isolated position. With the acquisition of the Philippine Islands, and the coming of the " spheres of influence " in China, the United States was forced to become an

[5] Jefferson's First Inaugural Address, Richardson, " Messages and Papers of the Presidents," I : 321–24.

active participant in Oriental politics. From now on, American diplomacy was what the Jeffersonian Republicans might have called aggressive imperialsm.

I

THE OPENING OF THE EAST

1. JAPAN

WHEN Commodore Perry reached Japan in 1853, he presented to the Emperor of Japan President Fillmore's letter asking for the friendship and commercial intercourse of the two nations. The American Government had long since wanted to open Japan to American trade. In 1815 Secretary Monroe had planned to send Commodore Porter to open Japan to trade. In 1837 the American ship *Morrison* had arrived in Yedo Bay, Japan, in hope of opening up trade, but had been driven away by bombardment. The motive of the American Government in its attempt to open Japan in 1853 was, as stated in President Fillmore's letter to the Japanese Emperor, " friendship, commerce, a supply of coal and provisions, and protection for our shipwrecked people." The American whale industry in the Pacific Ocean about this time was estimated at about $17,000,000. In several instances American whalers had been wrecked on the Japanese coasts and the crews had been maltreated by the Japanese officials, as in the case of the *Lawrence*

25

in 1846, and the *Ladoga* in 1848. Then, too, it was quite necessary for ocean liners plying between California and China to stop over in Japanese ports to provision themselves. In addition to all these material reasons, there was some sense of moral duty on the part of Christian America to open up heathen Japan to the penetrating rays of Christian civilization. Indeed, as early as 1816, John Quincy Adams urged the opening of Japan as a duty of Christian nations.

Between 1854, when the first American-Japanese treaty was signed at Yokohama, and 1899, when the Western nations recognized the full sovereignty of Dai Nippon, many significant historical events happened in the Sunrise Kingdom. It was during the early part of this period that the Japanese embassies returned from Europe and America with the astonishing discovery that " it is not the foreigners, but we ourselves who are barbarous." Japanese students were sent abroad to learn Western arts and sciences; foreign teachers were employed to reorganize the school system; the army was organized after the Western model, and the navy changed from fishermen's junks to iron-clad men-of-war; and feudal barons were forced to give up their powers to the central government. In short, Japan emerged from a state of mediæval feudalism into that of a modern constitutional monarchy, strongly centralized and highly efficient in its working order. In the Boxer uprising, 1900, she joined hands with the Western nations, and in the Russo-Japanese War, 1904-5, she completely surprised the world with the efficiency of her military organization. It was the first time since the Turk had pounded the gates of Vienna that a heathen nation of the East had shown itself able successfully to meet a Christian power of the West on the military field. With good reason did President Roosevelt pay high tribute in his message to Congress, 1906, to the spirit and methods of Japan in her acceptance and promotion of modern civilization; and it was largely through the instrumentality of President Roosevelt that the peace negotiations at Portsmouth were brought to a successful issue. When in 1908 Japan sent her first envoy, Viscount Shuzo Aoki, to the United States with the rank of Ambassador, it was the culmination of the long friendship between the two countries.

American relations with Japan in international questions have always been fair, and Japanese statesmen have looked up to the United States for moral support in their struggle for recognition by the Western Powers.[1] They

[1] The United States was the first of Western nations to withdraw the right of extra-territoriality from Japan by a treaty signed Nov. 22, 1894. See Part III.

knew the American lack of sinister designs in foreign lands, and had the utmost faith in the American sense of fair play, until the question of Japanese immigration and citizenship in America came up. This embarrassing question was complicated by discriminatory laws passed by some of the western states of the American Union—especially California—against aliens not qualified for citizenship. The labour element on the Pacific coast carried on a crusade against the Japanese on the grounds that the market for labour was cheapened by the presence of the Orientals. Politicians found a popular issue in vehement denunciations of the Japanese. For a time the Japanese question in California, serving as a football in local politics, furnished a source of grave complications between America and Japan.

It is not the purpose of this study to trace the historical relations between the United States and Japan, nor to deal with the Japanese problem within the United States. Many excellent volumes have been written on these topics.[2]

[2] On the historical relations between Japan and the United States, P. J. Treat, " Early Diplomatic Relations Between the United States and Japan; " John W. Foster, " American Diplomacy in the Orient; " W. E. Griffis, " America in the East; " J. M. Callahan, " American Relations in the Pacific and the Far East," are among the best accounts. For full treatment of the Japanese question in the United States, see : Sidney L. Gulick, " The American Japanese Problem; " K. K. Kawakami, " American Japanese Relations,

Suffice it to say here that the present friendship between the United States and Japan is largely traditional,[3] although the recent Imperial Commission headed by Viscount Ishii painted over the ugly spots of local friction with a fresh varnish of alliance against the " Common Enemy,"[4] and the Japanese question in the United States is still an unsettled issue.   No unbiased student of international relations will deny that a sovereign nation has a right to close its doors to undesirable immigrants, or that citizenship is a privilege to be granted and not a universal right to be claimed by every alien that comes to its shores.   But in the interest of fairness, the question presents itself, should the United States, the champion of world democracy, continue to deny its citizenship, which is open to all other races, including the blacks from the jungles of Africa, to Asiatics permanently settled in this country, who have educational and financial qualifications for all the duties and obligations of American citizenship?   The future affairs of the world must be settled by both the white *and*

Asia at the Door;" Harry Alvin Mills, " The Japanese Problem in the United States;" Lindsay Russell, " America to Japan;" Montaville Flowers, " Japanese Conquest of American Opinion;" J. F. Steiner, " The Japanese Invasion."

[3] Cf. K. K. Kawakami, " Japan and the United States," *Atlantic* 119:671–81, May, 1917.

[4] See Viscount Ishii's speeches during his visit in America, 1917, together with editorial comments on them by the American press.

the yellow races. Let it be known to the statesmen of the world—especially to the American
statesmen—that the ultimate welfare of the human race depends largely upon the wise ad-
justment of the relations between these two
dominant races, that the peace of the world
cannot be "planted upon the tested foundations of political liberty," unless this complicated problem is correctly solved. Surely the
American public should not, through indiffer-
ence, leave this problem to the hands of agitators and propagandists, when a lasting solution
can be made only in the light of its best reason
and highest wisdom.

2. Korea

Before passing to the Chinese question, it
might be worth our while to take a glance at the
closing chapter of the least known nation—once
a nation—in Asia.

The United States was the first Western
power to enter the gates of Korea.[6] The first
article of the Korean-American treaty signed at
Wonsan, Korea, May 22, 1882 (ratifications exchanged at Seoul, Korea, May 19, 1883), reads
as follows:

"There shall be perpetual peace and friendship between the President of the United States

[6] For early diplomatic intercourse between America and
Korea, see Foster, "American Diplomacy in the Orient,"
chap. IX.

and the King of Chosen and citizens and subjects of their respective governments. If other
powers deal unjustly or oppressively with either
government, the other will exert their good
offices, on being informed of the case, to bring
about an amicable arrangement, thus showing
their friendly feelings." *

Interpreting this diplomatic phraseology into
every-day language, it meant that America
would stand sponsor for the political independence and territorial integrity of Korea. And
the simple-minded Korean Government from
the Emperor down literally believed in it. In
fact, they had no reason to doubt the sincerity
of the United States. They saw the splendid
work of American philanthropy through missionary channels; the integrity of the American
Government was exemplified by the integrity of
American citizens there. They thought that
there was at least one great nation that was unselfish and honest and upon which they could
rely for support, as it was provided in the
Korean-American treaty, whenever their national life was in jeopardy. American citizens
were accorded greater privilege than any other
foreigners in Korea. The first Korean railway—Seoul-Chemulpo line—was built and
owned by an American concern; the first elec-

* Complete text of the treaty reprinted in *Senate Document*, No. 342, 64th Congress, 1st Session.

tric plant in Korea was installed by the Edison Company in 1895. The first and largest electric road and water works in Korea were built and owned by Americans.[1] The richest gold mine in Korea was given to an American firm. Dr. Horace N. Allen, former American minister to Korea, thus describes the gaining of the concession: "As the result of a long train of circumstances, it had become known to me exactly which district was considered the richest by the natives, and it was this district, twenty-five by thirty miles in extent, that I named in the concession."[2] It must be remembered that America did not get all these concessions from Korea by force as European nations got theirs in China. They were given to American concerns by the Korean Government in return for the good will and friendship of the United States.

Numerous other American industries in Korea might be mentioned, but it is enough to say that while Korea was an independent nation, the American business man had the best of the advantages open to foreigners in Korea. After mapping out her imperial program, and through the clever use of her publicity propaganda[3] Japan convinced the American public—espe-

[1] See Horace N. Allen, "Things Korean," chap. XIV; Thomas F. Millard, "The Far Eastern Question," chap. XII, "The Open Door in Korea."
[2] Allen, "Things Korean," pp. 232-233.
[3] See Part II.

cially official Washington—that she must have Korea in order to preserve peace in the Far East. " Japan began and carried through this whole matter," said Homer B. Hulbert, an American educator and for some time political adviser to the Korean Emperor, " by clever use of misinformation and broken promises, which successfully hoodwinked the American public." [10]

The first obvious step taken by the United States in handing Korea over to Japan was at the beginning of the Russo-Japanese War, when Japan violated Korean neutrality and exacted certain concessions from the Korean Government under " military necessity." The Secretary of State, John Hay, instructed the American minister at Seoul, Horace N. Allen, to observe strict neutrality and not cable the text of any agreement that Korea and Japan might come to." [11] This was undoubtedly done to avoid recognition of Korea's appeal against Japanese aggressions.

The next move the United States made to aid Japan in this game of Oriental politics was the recall of Dr. Allen from Korea. Dr. Allen had stayed in Korea over twenty years and was highly esteemed by both the natives and for-

[10] Homer B. Hulbert, " The Passing of Korea," p. 462.
[11] Cablegram sent from Washington, Feb. 23, 1904; recorded in *Senate Document*, No. 342 p. 11, 64th Congress, 1st Session.

eigners. When the Japanese began to tighten their grip in the peninsula, he told his government a few unpalatable truths about what the Japanese were doing in Korea. Immediately subtle influences were put in operation at Washington intimating that Minister Allen was a *persona non grata* to the Japanese. As a result Dr. Allen, despite his unquestioned integrity and long years of loyal service to his government, was summarily recalled, to the great surprise and indignation of American communities in Korea.

When hostilities began between Russia and Japan, America was officially neutral, but her sympathies were with Japan. There were three possible reasons for this: (1) Japan through her publicity propaganda created a favourable opinion of herself in America;[12] (2) Japan borrowed vast sums of money from America for war purposes, and Japanese success was naturally wished for by American capitalists; (3) at the beginning of the war Japan was thought of by the outside world as an " under-dog " trying to get loose from the brutal clutch of the Russian Bear. An incident which happened at Chemulpo Harbour immediately preceding the naval encounter of the two belligerents fur-

[12] For various methods of controlling American public opinion by Japan in regard to Japanese affairs, see Part II, "Japan's Control of Publicity." See also Flowers, "Japanese Conquest of American Opinion."

nishes an illuminating illustration of American
attitude toward the three nations directly concerned in the war,—Japan, Russia, and Korea.

On February 9, 1904, Admiral Uriu, the commander of the Japanese fleet, sent an ultimatum
to the captain of the *Variag*, the Russian war-
ship lying in the harbour of Chemulpo, that he
would give the Russian ships until twelve
o'clock to leave the harbour, and if they had not
moved by four o'clock that afternoon, the
Japanese fleet would come in and sink them at
their anchorage—in a neutral port of a neutral
country.

There were at that time in the harbour four
other foreign war-ships: the *Talbot* (British), the
Elba (Italian), the *Pascal* (French), and the
Vicksburg (American). The commander of the
British war-ship, notwithstanding the fact that
Great Britain was an ally of Japan, was indignant at the insolence of the Japanese Admiral,
and invited the commanders of the other foreign ships to a conference on board the *Talbot*
to decide what action should be taken. " The
British, French, and Italian commanders at once
decided that Admiral Uriu was proposing to
commit a gross breach of international law, and
they unanimously resolved to give the Russian
ships whatever protection they could. A message was sent to the commander of the *Variag*
informing him of this determination, and ad-

vising him to refuse to leave the harbour.[13] But the captain of the *Vicksburg* explained to the other commanders that he had received explicit instructions from his government to remain strictly neutral in the coming event. And the American war-ship *Vicksburg*, with its proud name, skulked into the inner harbour of safety. The Russian naval officers keenly resented this action of the *Vicksburg*, and the Russian press made bitter references to this incident as well as to the generally pro-Japanese tendency in America at that time as a breach of the historic friendship between America and Russia.[14]

At the time of the Portsmouth Conference between Russia and Japan, July, 1905, the Koreans in Hawaii sent their two delegates, Syngman Rhee and P. K. Yoon, to present a petition to President Roosevelt, asking that he " see to it that Korea may preserve her autonomous government." [15] The delegates were received unofficially, and their petition was given a sympathetic consideration. But this did not

[13] For full discussion of this incident, see Millard, " The New Far East," chap. V.

[14] Ever since the birth of the American nation, there has been no serious friction of any kind between the United States and Russia. During the Civil War the Russian fleet anchored outside the New York Harbour. It was generally understood, although not officially stated, that in case England and France took sides with the South, Russia would intervene on behalf of the North. Thus the Russian fleet gave no small moral support to the cause of the Union.

[15] See full text of the petition, Part III, I.

change the President's settled policy toward
Korea. When the Emperor of Korea sent
Homer B. Hulbert to present his letter to President Roosevelt asking for aid against Japan's
aggression, Mr. Hulbert was refused an inter-
view by both the President and Secretary of
State Root on one excuse after another until it
was too late.[16] "So far from pleading the case
of Korea with Japan, America was the first to
fall in with and give its open assent to the
destruction of the old administration. On the
first intimation from Japan it agreed, without
inquiry and with almost indecent haste, to withdraw its minister from Seoul."[17]

When the United States declared neutrality
at the beginning of the recent European war,
the very men who ignored treaty obligations
and handed over, as far as America was concerned, the "Belgium of the East" to Japan,
Theodore Roosevelt and Elihu Root, were the
loudest in denouncing the Wilson Administration for not going to war against Germany in
defense of Belgian neutrality. There was no
treaty binding upon the United States to defend
Belgium against the unrighteous aggressor as in
the case of Korea. The Democratic President
and Congress retaliated by publishing the ac-

[16] For a full description of Hulbert's mission, see Part
III, J, "American Policy in the Cases of Korea and Belgium."
[17] F. A. McKenzie, "Tragedy of Korea," p. 131.

counts of the Roosevelt and Root Administration ignoring Korea's appeal in the last days
of her struggle against Japan.[18] For the first
time the part played, or not played, by the
United States in that tragedy in the Far East
came to light. When newspaper reporters interviewed Root on the subject, he refused to
comment on it. Alvey A. Adee, who was the
Second Assistant Secretary of State under Root,
and who is the star witness of the Korean case
at Washington, also refused to comment on the
matter, but said, " It is ancient history, anyhow."[19]

Korea was the bone of contention of the East
for a number of years. It was only through a
favourable combination of circumstances that
Japan was enabled to occupy it. Russia gave
her consent to Japanese occupation as her war
indemnity; England welcomed the expansion of
her ally's influence on the mainland of Asia to
checkmate the Russian advance and to protect
the British interests in the East, so that she
might concentrate her navy in the North Sea to
counteract Germany. But the United States,
instead of gaining something by the " deal,"
lost all the advantages she had held before. Before the Russo-Japanese War, American business men enjoyed the largest share of foreign

[18] *Senate Document,* No. 342, 64th Congress, 1st Session.
[19] *New York Times,* March 6, 1916.

trade in Korea and Manchuria.[20]   But now their place is taken by Japanese. The American policy then, as now, was not motivated by material gains. The statesmen at Washington were convinced that Korea was utterly " incapable of independence "—the same kind of conviction that Metternich had toward Italy, George III toward American colonies, and the statesmen of the Central Powers toward Serbia, Belgium, and all the constituent states of Austria-Hungary. The principle of " no people must be forced under sovereignty under which it does not wish to live " [21] was as yet too far off an ideal to be a common expression of American statesmen.

The Korean people learned too late that there is no such a thing as international honesty, and that treaty obligations backed by no force are not worth the paper upon which they are written. The United States was the first of Western nations to enter Korea, the first to enjoy the preferential treatment and commercial advantages in that land, and the first to desert her in the time of her dire need of American friendship. Dr. Allen well sums up the case of Korean-American treaty obligations in the following words:

[20] See Allen, " Things Korean," pp. 215, ff.
[21] From President Wilson's Message to Russia, May 26. 1917.

" Korea has taken that treaty to mean just what the words say, while we seem to have utterly disregarded the solemn promise we therein voluntarily made, that we would lend her our good offices should she be oppressed by a third power; thus breaking faith with a people who trusted us implicitly, and who consented to the opening of her doors on this guarantee of friendly aid." [22]

Thus the United States of America " sneered at freedom and lent arms to the tyrant " in the demolition of a civilization that began long before David became the king of Israel.[23]

3.   China

A prominent Western historian and scientist won distinction for a time by his advocacy of a novel idea that a nation, like an individual, has its infancy, maturity, senility, and final extinction.[24]   This idea was supported by a few superficial observers of Oriental politics who maintained that the Eastern nations had long since reached the summit of their evolution, and that no further progress in the future was to be ex-

[22] Allen, " Things Korean," p. 214.
[23] For antiquity of Korean civilization, see W. E. Griffis, " Corea—The Hermit Nation " ; H. B. Hulbert, " The Passing of Korea."
[24] See John William Draper, " History of the Intellectual Development of Europe."

pected.[25] Interesting though these theories may be, they have little historical foundation. A nation may have ebbs and flows of civilization in the cycle of its life, but there is no reason for its predestined maturity and decay except through its adoption of wrong institutions. Egypt in Africa, Italy in Europe, and China in Asia furnish ample evidences to upset the theory of an analogy between the life of a nation and that of an individual.

When China opened her gates to the treaty powers of the West, her civilization was at its ebb. The China that Marco Polo found in the thirteenth century was undoubtedly in a higher stage of civilization than the China of the nineteenth century. The " foreign-devil " notion and the spirit of exclusiveness were not the attitude of China toward foreigners in the Middle Ages. On the contrary, the alien then enjoyed in China rights and privileges such as he could enjoy in few, if any, countries of modern times. " The imperial government placed the aliens practically on the same footing as its own subjects: it opened to them public employments and extended to them the fullest protection. Olopun, one of the Nestorians who entered China in the Tang Dynasty, was raised to the

[25] See Henry Sumner Maine's "Ancient Law" and his theory of progressive and non-progressive races together with the theories advanced by his followers along the same line.

rank of high priest and national protector by Emperor Kautsung. Marco Polo, though a Venetian by birth, was appointed to the office of prefect of Yangchow, which he held for three years." [26]

When the Portuguese first entered the Canton River in 1517, they were received in a kindly spirit. But their greedy and high-handed methods in their relations with the natives turned the feeling of amity into one of hatred, and caused the Ming Emperor in 1545 to issue an edict to attack the foreigners. The Spaniards made their appearance in 1575, but they were as cruel and greedy as the Portuguese, and failed to restore the prestige of Westerners in the eyes of the Chinese. The successive events of European expansion in the East,—the conquest of the East Indies, and the forcible occupation of parts of India and the Malay Peninsula by Portuguese adventurers,—awakened the suspicions of the Chinese as to the ulterior motives of the foreigners rapidly flocking to their shores. At this early period of European intercourse, China unfortunately received a bad impression that all Europeans were barbarians and adventurers.

Commercial relations between England and China began in 1635, when Captain John Weddell was sent to China with a small fleet of

[26] V. K. W. Koo, "The Status of Aliens in China," p. 19.

vessels. Later two missions—one under the Earl of Macartney in 1793, and the other under Lord Amherst in 1816—were sent to China from England for the purpose of arriving at a better understanding in regard to the trade relations between the two countries. Lord Napier was appointed as Commercial Superintendent of the British Government in China in 1833, when the control of the British trade at Canton passed out of the hands of the East India Company. All the British had accomplished during the two hundred years of commercial intercourse with China was the establishment of a trading post in Canton. Their attempt to enter into a cordial relationship with China on the basis of international comity and mutual understanding had been a complete failure. The Chinese continued to suspect the motive of the foreigner and treated him as a barbarian. This suspicion and hatred was intensified when opium was forced upon China through the muzzles of the British men-of-war, and the Chinese Government was compelled to submit to the demands of the British.[27]

The treaty of Nanking, signed at the close of

[27] The treaty was signed in 1842 at the close of the "Opium War." By this treaty, the island of Hongkong was ceded to Great Britain, an indemnity was paid for the opium destroyed, official correspondence was to be carried on on equal terms, and Canton, Amoy, Foochow, Ningpo, and Shanghai were opened to foreign trade as treaty ports, where foreigners could reside.

the first Anglo-Chinese War, did not settle all the pending issues between the Chinese and the British. The constant friction between the Chinese and the British officials in regard to their respective rights, and the continuance of opium smuggling by the British merchants at Canton and Hongkong, furnished causes for another war. This time the French, actuated partly by the desire to seek reparation for the massacre of a missionary in West Kwangsi, and partly by the spirit of imperial aggrandizement, joined with the English in war against China. The allied forces took Canton, and then carried war to the north. The Chinese were forced to sue for peace, and the war was brought to a close by the treaty of Tientsin, signed June 26, 1859. The treaty provided among other things the right of residence by foreign ministers in Peking, the opening of five additional treaty ports, and the toleration of the Christian religion.[78] The Chinese, later on, tried to evade the carrying out of these provisions. This caused the allied armies to make an expedition to Peking, where they burned the Summer Palace as a punitive measure, and compelled the Chinese Government to sign another treaty on October 22, 1860. In addition to the terms of

---

[78] At this time the United States and Russia also made treaties with China, although they took no part in the conflict.

the treaty of Tientsin, Kowloon was ceded to the British and Tientsin was opened as a treaty port. Foreign ministers for the first time took up their residence in Peking, Anson Burlingame representing the United States.[29]

Repeated defeats and humiliations caused the Chinese Government to make feeble attempts at reform. In 1867 the first Chinese embassy was sent to foreign countries for the purpose of winning for China more favourable treatment from Western nations. The embassy was headed by Anson Burlingame, who had completed his term as the first American minister to China. This was the beginning of American prestige in the Far East. Minister Burlingame, through his personal integrity and diplomatic foresight, won the respect and confidence of the Chinese. He convinced the Chinese Government that his country of all Western nations had no ulterior motives in Chinese territory.[30] The most notable achievement of the embassy was the conclusion of the treaty of 1868 with the United States. " It stipulated the territorial integrity of China by disavowing any right to interfere with its eminent domain or sovereign jurisdiction over

---

[29] For Burlingame's career as the American minister to China, see U. S. " Diplomatic Correspondence," 1862-68, China; Martin's " Cathay," pt. II, chap. II.

[30] See U. S. " Diplomatic Correspondence," 1868, pt. I, pp. 493, 502, 601; 1870, pp. 317, 332; 1871, p. 166; Martin's " Cathay," p. 374; Speer's " China," p. 429.

its subjects and property; it recognized the
right of China to regulate its internal trade not
affected by treaty; provided for the appointment of consuls; secured exemption from persecution or disability on account of religion;
recognized the right of voluntary emigration;
pledged the privilege of residence and travel in
either country on the basis of most favoured
nation; granted the privilege of schools and
colleges; disavowed the intention to interfere
in the domestic administration of China in respect to public improvements, but expressed
the willingness of the United States to aid in
such enterprise when requested by China." [31]

All these outward signs of change and reform
did not affect the core of China. The depths of
Chinese conservatism were like those of a vast
ocean undisturbed by the surface ripples of wars
and treaties. The *literati* of China were as firm
as ever in their belief that China was the center
of the world's culture—hence the name, "Middle
Kingdom"—and that all the foreign nations
were barbarians. When the first imperial
audience for foreign ambassadors was held in

---

[31] Foster, "American Diplomacy in the Orient," pp. 365–
366. The voluntary emigration clause of this treaty was
revised later, and exclusion laws were passed against Chinese
labourers. For voluminous findings of investigating com-
mittees, debates in Congress, editorial comments pro and con
on the subject, see " Select List of References on Chinese
Immigration," compiled by A. P. C. Griffin, Library of Congress, Washington, 1904.

Peking in 1873, it took place in the "Pavilion
of Purple Light," a hall used for receiving
tributary nations. Something decidedly violent
was needed to stir the complacency of the
Chinese and upset their naïve attitude of
superiority. Now Japan was ready to play her
rôle in Eastern politics.

For centuries China considered Korea as a
vassal nation[32] and Japan as an archipelago of
barbarous tribes. Japan patiently forebore the
insolence of China during the early period of
Meiji Era with the anticipation of coming back
at her later. After the internal troubles were
settled and the country was thoroughly organized on a modern basis, the Japanese statesmen
launched the program of imperial expansion,
and hastened military and naval preparations
with astonishing rapidity for what they deemed
to be the inevitable conflict with China. When
they thought they were sufficiently prepared,
they struck the blow in 1894, and China was
completely prostrated.[33]

[32] Korea had her autonomy in all its essentials. Dynasties
changed, wars and treaties were made with foreign countries
without regard to China. See Bishop, "Korea and Her
Neighbours"; Griffis, "Corea—The Hermit Nation"; Longford, "The Story of Korea"; McKenzie, "The Tragedy of
Korea"; Hulbert, "The History of Korea."

[33] For the causes of the war, see Sengman Rhee, "The
Spirit of Korean Independence," pp. 164–173 (Korean);
"U. S. Foreign Relations," 1894, Appendix I, pp. 5–23;
Williams, "History of China," pp. 437–444; Griffis, "Corea,"
pp. 460–462; Henry Norman, "The People and Politics of

The United States performed an important mission during and at the close of the war. When the war was declared, both belligerent countries intrusted the archives and property of their legations and consulates and the interests of their subjects in the enemy country to the care of the United States ministers and consuls in the respective countries. At the close of the conflict, peace overtures were made through American ministers both at Peking and Tokyo.[34] Thus the United States proved herself a disinterested friend to both China and Japan, and established the foundation for further diplomatic achievements in the East. The Emperor of Japan, soon after the close of the war, sent a letter to the President of the United States expressing his cordial thanks for the good offices of the United States during the war. A similar sentiment was expressed by China through Li Hung Chang on his visit to the United States in 1896.[35]

the Far East," pp. 259–266; Curzon, "Far East," pp. 196–208.

For the events of the war, see "Foreign Relations," 1894, Appendix I, pp. 44–104; Williams, "China," pp. 444–459; "Vladimir," "The China-Japan War," London, 1896, pts. II and III, Appendix D, F-H. For results of the war, see J. H. Wilson, U. S. A., "China, Travels in the Middle Kingdom," chap. XX.

[34] For peace negotiations, see "Foreign Relations," 1894, Appendix I, pp. 29–106; 1895, p. 969; "History of Peace Negotiations Between China and Japan," officially revised, Tientsin, 1895; Williams, "China," p. 459.

[35] See "Memoirs of Li Hung Chang," edited by W. F. Mannix, Shanghai, 1912.

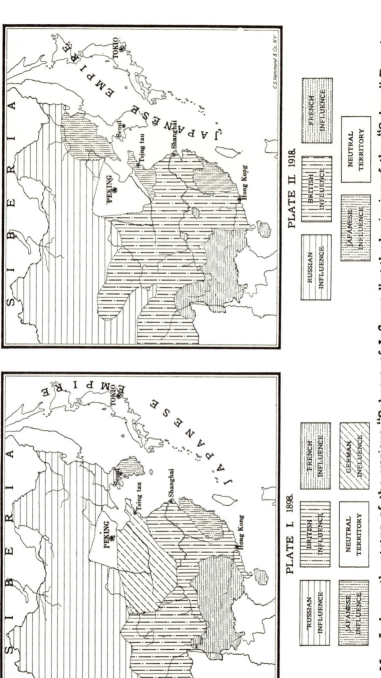

PLATE I. 1898.

| RUSSIAN INFLUENCE | BRITISH INFLUENCE | FRENCH INFLUENCE |
| JAPANESE INFLUENCE | NEUTRAL TERRITORY | GERMAN INFLUENCE |

PLATE II. 1918.

| RUSSIAN INFLUENCE | JAPANESE INFLUENCE | BRITISH INFLUENCE | FRENCH INFLUENCE |
| | | NEUTRAL TERRITORY | |

C.S. Hammond & Co., N.Y.

Map I shows the status of the various "Spheres of Influence" at the beginning of the "Sphere" Doctrine (about 1898). Map II illustrates the growth of Japanese influence on the Asiatic Mainland (chiefly China and Korea) subsequent to the Russo-Japanese and the recent European Wars. The United States has no "Sphere."

II

CHINA IN THE TWENTIETH CENTURY

1. "Spheres of Influence" vs "Open Door"

THE position of China at the opening of the twentieth century was peculiar. The China-Japanese War, 1894–95, revealed the utter helplessness of China. When the three European powers—Germany, France, and Russia—sent a notice to Japan to withdraw from the mainland of Asia and to return to China the conquered territory of the Liaotung Peninsula, they did not do so with the altruistic motive of helping China preserve her territorial integrity. Their action was motivated, as was proved by subsequent events, by a desire to curb the expansion of Japanese influence on the Asiatic mainland, and to appropriate for themselves, in time, what Japan wanted as a prize of her victory. The downfall of China was predicted, and the partition of that vast empire among civilized nations was freely discussed. Then arose the "sphere of influence" doctrine. This peculiar modern doctrine, paraphrased, means that each nation that has some interest in China shall map out a certain district as its own sphere in which it will have a paramount influence, and out of which other nations must stay. In case of final partition, each district thus mapped out will become a territory of its respective owner. Even in far-off China, as in Europe proper, the spirit of European rivalry was based on the theory and practice of balance of power. And every incident was utilized as a pretext to press upon the Chinese Government claims for leases, concessions, and privileges of one kind or another.

Germany fired the opening gun in this European lease scramble in China. In 1897 two German missionaries were killed by a Chinese mob. The German Government lost no time in seizing this opportunity. German men-of-war appeared promptly in Kiaochow Bay, occupied the city, demanded, as an indemnity, the lease of Kiaochow for ninety-nine years, and the recognition of a German sphere of influence in the greater part of Shantung Peninsula. These demands were complied with by the Chinese Government in the treaty signed March 8, 1898.

This move of Germany turned loose the pent-up ambition of European nations to exploit China. Russia, who had already held railroad franchises in northern Manchuria, now approached China with cajolery, intimidation, and promises of aid in case of further aggression by other European nations,[1] and succeeded in leasing Port Arthur, Talienwan, and the adjacent waters as naval bases. The Manchurian Railway Company under Russian control was given the right to construct a branch line to Port Arthur. England forced China to sign a lease of Weihaiwei together with the adjacent waters, July 1, 1898. In like manner France occupied Kwangchow Bay under a ninety-nine year lease; and Italy obtained the right to develop the port of Sanmun. In April, 1898, England and Russia made an agreement that Russia should have her sphere of influence to the north of the Great Wall of China, and England to have hers to the south.

The movement for the partition of China was thus well under way. Unless some counteracting influence was introduced, China no longer could maintain her national entity. The United States with her newly acquired insular possessions in the East could not afford to be indifferent to the partition of China. There were two courses open to her: She had either to deviate entirely from her traditional foreign policy and seize her share of land and commercial advantages in China, regardless of justice and fairness to the Chinese, or to exercise her

[1] For Russian intrigues in China, see Rhee, " The Spirit of Korean Independence," pp. 173, ff.

good offices to preserve the integrity of the Chinese Empire.   She chose the nobler way.

On September 6, 1899, the Secretary of State, John Hay, addressed notes to England, Germany, and Russia, and later to France, Italy, and Japan, declaring the "open door" doctrine in China.[2] This formal protest of the United States in behalf of China requested the Powers to give their official assurances to the effect: (1) that they would not interfere with any treaty port or vested interest in their respective spheres of influence; (2) that the Chinese tariff should continue to be collected by Chinese officials; (3) that they would not discriminate against other foreigners in the matter of port dues or railroad rates.[3] England expressed her willingness to sign such a declaration, and other powers, while carefully avoiding to commit themselves, showed their accord with the principles set forth by Mr. Hay. These principles, together with the principle of the territorial and

[2] For full discussion of diplomatic intercourse between the United States and other powers and the part played by John Hay, consult W. R. Thayer, "Life and Letters of John Hay," 2 vols., 1915.

[3] This doctrine is being violated by Japanese in Manchuria now. Japanese merchants through government subsidies, special railway rebates, preferential customs treatment, and exemption from internal taxation, have monopolized the Manchurian market. Consult Millard, "The Far Eastern Question," chaps. XV–XX; Hollington K. Tong, "American Money and Japanese Brains in China," *Review of Reviews*, 53:452–455, April, 1916; "Japan, China, and American Money," *Harper's Weekly*, 62:298–299, March 25, 1916.

administrative integrity of China, were empha-
sized by the American Government in the settlement of the Boxer trouble in China, and since
then the principle of the " open door " in China
has become an American doctrine, recognized as
such by the Powers just as the time-honoured
Monroe Doctrine is recognized.

2. THE BOXER UPRISING

The rapid foreign exploitation of Chinese
territory, the introduction of Christianity into
China, the constant bullying of the natives by
foreigners, aroused the Chinese to concerted
action. To the fogyish Chinese mind, everything foreign was repulsive. They could not
distinguish the work of an American missionary
from the opium traffic of a British merchant.
The only way, they thought, that they could
enjoy again the undisturbed peace of the old
times was to drive all the " foreign devils " out
of the country. Prince Tuan, an influential
reactionary, formed an organization known as
the Society of Boxers to expel all foreigners
from China. This movement was secretly encouraged by the Empress Dowager, who was
holding the supreme power in China after the
coup d'état in 1898, and by all the reactionary
officials under her. The movement spread like
wild-fire, and the army of Boxers joined by imperial forces occupied Peking. Foreign repre-

sentatives fled to the British Legation. Many tragic incidents occurred to both the Chinese and the foreigners in China during the struggle.[4] Promptly an expeditionary force composed of English, French, German,[5] Russian, Japanese, and American soldiers marched to Peking and lifted the siege. The imperial court fled westward, and later appointed Li Hung Chang as its representative to negotiate with the Powers.

This was the most critical period of Chinese history in recent times. China had incurred "well-nigh universal indignation," as Minister Wu expressed it, when he was presenting a cablegram from his emperor to President McKinley, asking for American aid in settling her difficulties with the Powers. The Powers, with good reason, looked upon the Chinese Government as hostile, and many of them—especially Russia—were willing to consent to the partition of China. But the United States insisted on regarding the outrages as the work of insurrectionists, and remained on friendly terms with the constituted authorities, thus firmly upholding the territorial and administrative integrity

[4] For full account of the Boxer War, consult Paul Henry Clemants, "The Boxer Rebellion," Columbia University Studies in History, Economics, and Public Law, vol. 66, 1915; Rhee, "Spirit of Korean Independence," pp. 175, ff.; "Foreign Relations," 1900, pp. 77, ff.

[5] The German troops remained at Kiaochow and took no part in the expedition, although the allied forces were led by Field-Marshal Count von Waldersee chosen as Generalissimo to satisfy the Kaiser.

of China. Then, too, many a wise statesman in the world saw a condition of general anarchy and the possibility of world war over the spoils, in case China were partitioned. It was much better for a nation like England, which enjoyed the largest foreign trade in China, to restore the *status quo*, and enjoy the commercial privileges, than to take the chance of losing them by partition. Thus the Powers finally followed the lead of the United States in preserving China as a nation and maintaining there the principle of the " open door."

The final protocol settling the difficulties consequential to the Boxer Uprising was signed on September 7, 1901. China agreed: (1) to punish those who were responsible for and who took part in foreign massacres; (2) to adopt adequate measures to prevent recurrence of such disorders; (3) to indemnify the losses sustained by foreign nations and individuals; (4) to improve trade relation with foreign nations.

During the lengthy negotiation prior to the signing of this protocol the United States threw the weight of its influence on the side of moderation, urging the powers not to make the burden too heavy for China. The total indemnity ($333,000,000 approximately) imposed upon China was far in excess of the actual losses sustained by the powers. The share that was assigned to the United States was a little over

$24,000,000, whereas the actual loss sustained by the American Government and its citizens was only about $11,000,000. Once more the American Government deviated from the grab-it-all spirit of modern diplomacy, and in 1907 returned the amount in excess of actual losses. The Chinese Government, in return, sent Tang Shao Yi as its special envoy to thank the United States, and decided to use the money thus returned by the American Government to educate Chinese students in American colleges and universities.[6] This step taken by the American Government was an act of simple justice, and it remains to be seen whether the European Powers who took advantage of China's prostration to demand far heavier indemnities than their claims justified will yet take similar action.[7]

3. THE RUSSO-JAPANESE STRUGGLE

After the protocol was signed, other nations withdrew their forces from China, but Russia retained her forces in Manchuria and gradually strengthened her position in eastern China. She not only retained all vantages gained prior to and during the Boxer Uprising, but was

[6] There were 679 Chinese students (male alone) in American colleges and universities in 1916, according to the *Directory of Foreign Students,* published by the Committee on Friendly Relations Among Foreign Students, International Y. M. C. A., New York City.

[7] *Washington Post,* June 19, 1907; opinion of Judge Charles Sumner Lobinger of the American Court in Shanghai, China, *Nebraska State Journal,* October 11, 1917.

secretly pressing upon the Chinese Government for further concessions. This serious situation led to the Anglo-Japanese Alliance of 1902 to put a check upon Russian influence. The United States entered a formal protest at Petrograd and succeeded in getting a definite promise from the Russian Government not to oppose the opening of two Manchurian cities, Mukden and Antung, to foreign commerce by China. This did not, however, check the outstretching clutch of the Northern Bear, and Russian influence in Manchuria kept on increasing.

Japan was now ready to make an active resistance. Her attempts to negotiate with Russia the question of neutrality and the " open door " in Manchuria and China were fruitless.[8] Feeling that she was strong enough to combat her rival, and that the Anglo-Japanese Alliance safeguarded her from the attack of a third power in alliance with Russia, she struck the first blow on February 10, 1904. Secretary Hay promptly sent identical notes to Russia and to Japan, expressing the wish of the United States that the neutrality and administrative entity of China should be respected by the belligerents. In reply both Russia and Japan agreed to re-

[8] For the complete diplomatic correspondence between Russia and Japan prior to the opening of hostility, see " Russo-Japanese War," published by Collier & Son, New York.

spect Chinese neutrality outside of Manchuria. On January 10, 1905, Hay addressed circular notes to the powers to the effect that it was the wish of the United States that the war would not result in any concession of Chinese territory. This note met with the hearty approval of Germany, Austria-Hungary, France, Great Britain, and Italy.

The greatest single stroke of diplomacy that established American dignity and prestige in the Pacific basin since the declaration of the " open door " doctrine, was the mediation of President Roosevelt on behalf of the two belligerent nations. Russia was completely prostrated, and Japan, though victorious, was at the end of her financial resources. On June 8, 1905, President Roosevelt made a formal appeal in the interest of the civilized world to the emperors of Japan and Russia to cease hostilities and open direct negotiations. Both nations complied with the request and sent their envoys to the United States to open a peace conference. The conference began its regular sessions at Portsmouth, New Hampshire, on August 8th, and the treaty was signed September 5th. More than once during the negotiations, the envoys came to points of controversy and were unable to reach an agreement. The Russian commission was headed by the astute diplomat, Count Witte, who made a most favourable impression and drew to himself the sympathetic interest of the public. In presenting the cause of his country, he capitalized the situation created by his striking personality. He conceded every demand made by Japan, but refused to pay a single ruble of indemnity. President Roosevelt unofficially advised, restrained, and urged the envoys to compromise their differences. Russia finally agreed to recognize Japan's paramount interest in Korea; to transfer, with the consent of China, her lease of Port Arthur, Talienwan, and adjacent territories to Japan; and to evacuate Manchuria and leave its doors wide open to the trade of the world.

By the result of this conference Japan, perhaps, got as much as she had expected, although not as much as she wanted. The Japanese envoys went home somewhat disgruntled—at least outwardly so—and when they reached home they had to have police protection from howling mobs. Japanese dailies made bitter comments to the effect that Japan won all the battles in the war, and lost all the spoils on the green table. Later, when the anti-American feeling was high as an echo of the anti-Japanese sentiment in California, more than one periodical in Japan referred to the diplomatic "loss" sustained by Japan at the Portsmouth conference as the result of American intervention.

The close of the Russo-Japanese War marks

the beginning of new political relations between the East and the West. Up to this time the Western nations—especially the United States— looked upon the East with sympathetic regard. But now, one of the nations of the effete East had proved herself equal to a Western Power in the field of military operations, and able to give as well as take blows. From now on the West must necessarily change its attitude toward the East from that of patronage to one of recognition on the basis of honour and equality. The United States has the proud distinction of having opened Japan and Korea to modern civilization, and of having saved China from disintegration after the Boxer rebellion. Japan knew the honourable intentions of the United States in the Orient, and looked up to her for moral support in her struggle for recognition from the Western Powers. And the United States regarded Japan as one of her brightest protégés and took pride in having played such an important part in bringing a secluded mediæval nation up to the first rank among the modern civilized nations. All this era of good feeling and mutual trust ended with the Portsmouth conference. Henceforth Japan was to be a rival of the United States in the theater of Eastern commerce and politics. Japan, a new recruit in the field of commercial and political expansion of the world, must necessarily infringe upon the rights of the pioneer nations of the West, including the United States, in order to realize her dream of greatness. And the United States, for the safeguarding of its interests, was compelled to lay certain restrictions upon Japan, such as restriction of Japanese immigration into the United States and its insular possessions, and vindication of the principles of the " open door " and the political integrity of China. Japan in turn resented these restrictions as an obstruction of her imperial progress. But she is at present in no position to make a vigorous protest to the United States. Economically, the United States is her second best customer, China being the first; and from a military standpoint, the United States is far superior both in man-power and in resources. Japan feels that she must " eat worms " for the time being. She prefers to have all negotiations not satisfactory to her postponed indefinitely until such time when she will be in a position to make demands as well as to make " appeals." She must be content to cover her wounds with diplomatic grace. In 1914, when Secretary Bryan handed the American reply to the Japanese note concerning the pending California Alien Law question, Ambassador Chinda said, " Will this be final? " Secretary Bryan replied, " There is nothing final between friends."

III

AMERICAN RIVALRY WITH JAPAN

1. THE AMERICAN FLEET IN THE FAR EAST

SUBSEQUENT American policies in the Far East have been along the path laid down by John Hay. The Root-Takahira agreement exchanged at Washington, November 30, 1908, outlined the mutual position of the United States and Japan regarding China as follows: (1) to encourage the free and peaceful development of their commerce on the Pacific; (2) to maintain the *status quo* in the Pacific, and to preserve the principle of equal commercial opportunity in China; (3) to reciprocally " respect the territorial possessions belonging to each other in said region "; (4) to preserve and maintain the independence and integrity of China; (5) the two governments will communicate with each other in case the *status quo* or the principle of equal opportunity is threatened as above defined.

It was not a formal treaty but merely an agreement—a " gentlemen's agreement "—rely-

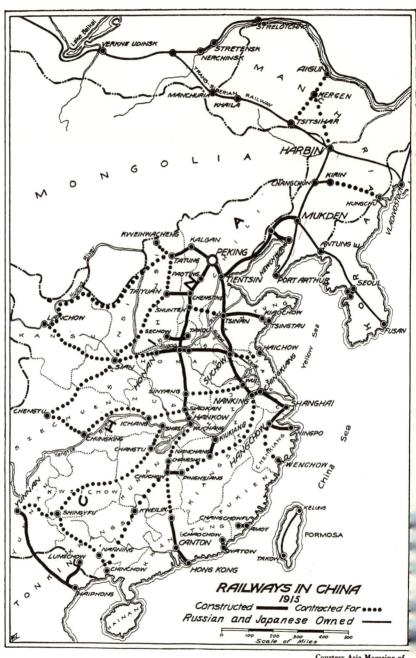

RAILWAYS IN CHINA
1915
Constructed ▬▬▬   Contracted For ••••
Russian and Japanese Owned ▬▬▬

Scale of Miles
0   100   200   300   400   500

ing upon the mutual trust and honour of the contracting parties for the observance of its provisions. Japan was anxious to convince the United States that she had no sinister designs on the mainland of Asia, and the United States was desirous of assuring Japan that the result of the Russo-Japanese War did not change the " open door " status in China. American policy toward both China and Japan has always been non-aggressive. In trying to befriend both, the United States has, unintentionally, in minor matters, played into the hands of the more clever and aggressive of the two nations. The visit of the American fleet to Asiatic waters in 1908 may be cited as illustration of this.

In 1907 when President Roosevelt decided to send the American fleet around the world, the Chinese were anxious to have the fleet pay a visit to China. They had looked up to the United States for moral support, if not active assistance, in their struggle for national stability. Their attitude was not without foundation. During the Boxer settlement, the United States was China's one friend among the nations of the West, and it was through American effort that a degree of moderation in the demands made was secured. In October, 1907, Secretary of War William Howard Taft said in his speech at Shanghai that " the United States and others who sincerely favour the ' open door ' policy

will, if they are wise, not only welcome, but
encourage this great Chinese Empire to take
long steps in administrative and governmental
reforms, in the development of her natural resources and the improvement of the welfare of
her people."[1] This statement, though unofficially made, assumed somewhat of an official
nature, as it was from a great American statesman who was to be the next president of his
country and as it was made before a large
gathering of both foreigners and Chinese in
that great metropolis of the East.   The Chinese
wished to reciprocate the good will of America
in refunding the balance of Boxer indemnity, by
welcoming the American fleet to their shores.

As soon as this move in China was known at
Tokyo, action was taken with the characteristic
Japanese celerity to checkmate the Chinese attempt to gain American favour and recognition.
The Japanese Government immediately dispatched an invitation which reached Washington one day ahead of that of the Chinese Government.   Subtle influences were exerted to
defeat Chinese expectations.   The Japanese had
apparently three reasons for their attempt to
frustrate the plans of the Chinese Government
in inviting the American fleet to Chinese waters:

[1] Secretary Taft was welcomed at Shanghai, China, October 8, 1907, " The World's Almanac and Encyclopedia," 1908,
p. 314.

(1) After the war with Russia the Japanese had created among the Oriental nations an impression that their fighting force was equal, if not superior, to that of any Western nation, and they did not want a first-class foreign fleet to anchor off Chinese waters and destroy that impression. (2) They wanted to make the Oriental peoples feel that Japan was the only Asiatic nation recognized on the basis of equality by Western Powers; and if the American fleet visited both Japan and China it would elevate China to the same plane with Japan. (3) The Japanese wanted to keep the relation between China and the United States as distant and non-intimate as possible, so that they could allude to China as a backward nation that must need the tutelage of Japan, while to China they could intimate that her aspirations for recognition and equal treatment by Western Powers were useless except through Japan, and that, indeed, China's solution of her national problems must be in following Japanese leadership.

European residents in China, who were none too eager to have American prestige in China and the cordial relation between China and the United States enhanced, heartily encored Japanese sentiment. Through W. W. Rockhill, the American minister to China, who was then in Japan on his way back from America, official Washington was informed of the inadvisability of sending a fleet to China. The original plan was revised and a part of the American fleet visited Amoy instead of Shanghai—the original city designated by both the Chinese and American residents in China for the welcome of the fleet. This was a great disappointment to both the Chinese and the Americans in China, who had planned an elaborate welcome to the fleet in the greatest center of communication and commerce in the East. The " number two fleet and number two admiral are coming to China, while the number one fleet and number one admiral are going to Japan," said the Chinese papers. All their enthusiasm was dampened, and the reception was perfunctory. The news of the Chinese reception of the American fleet was scattered abroad through the channels of Japanese publicity as being cold and unappreciative, and as showing the backward condition of China.

2. AMERICAN AND BRITISH POLICIES

With the incoming of the Taft and Knox administration, the American policy in the Orient assumed a more active form. Both President Taft and Secretary of State Knox had some knowledge of what was taking place in the East subsequent to the Russo-Japanese War. After singeing the outstretching paws of the Northern Bear, Japan occupied her place in the sun with other first-class Powers of the world, and was ready to play the rôle of mistress of Asia. England's fear and suspicion of Russian domination in the East, which had been the nightmare of English statesmen for the past half a century, now faded away. In place of the Russian phantom stalked the ever-threatening figure of the German Superman with *Kultur* in one hand and *Weltpolitik* in the other. German industries were monopolizing the markets of the world by both business efficiency and " dumping," and the German navy was growing by leaps and bounds.[2]

In the Anglo-Russian rivalry it had been merely a question of protecting British possessions and commercial interests in the East; but now the very existence of the British Empire was threatened by the *Weltpolitik*. English statesmen realized the vital need of readjustment of their policy to meet changed conditions. They buried the hatchet with Russia by allowing her a free hand in Mongolia in return for the safeguarding of British interests in China.

[2] Many excellent books have been written on *Kultur, Weltpolitik,* growth of the German navy, " dumping," Anglo-German rivalry, etc., leading up to the war. The following are a few typical references: Reventlow, " Deutschland's auswartige Politik"; Tardieu, " France and the Alliances," von Bülow, " Imperial Germany " ; Bernhardi, " Germany and the Next War " ; Rohrbach, " Der Deutsche Gedanke in der Welt " ; Dawson, " Evolution of Modern Germany " ; Price, " Diplomatic History of the War of 1914"; publications of various governments engaged in the war.

In European politics, Russia and Great Britain regarded each other as allies; and in matters of Asiatic policy they coöperated, as illustrated in the division of Persia into spheres of influence assumed by their respective governments.[3] The Anglo-Japanese Alliance of 1902, defensive in character, was renewed in 1905 and again in 1911. Japan promised to protect British possessions in Asia, and Great Britain in turn consented to the free hand of the Japanese in Manchuria, and to support Japan,—or at least, not to oppose her,—in whatever measures she deemed necessary in firmly establishing her sphere on the mainland of Asia. England also settled all differences with France on an amicable basis, supported her against Germany in the Moroccan question in 1907, and formed an entente to offset the Triple Alliance.[4] The protection of British interests in the Mediterranean was left to the French just as the possessions in the East were left to the care of the Japanese. Thus the British fleet was able to concentrate in the North Sea to meet any exigency that might occur, and to bottle up the German fleet

[3] The Anglo-Russian Agreement of August 31, 1907, regarding Persia has never been made public. See *Review of Reviews*, 45:49-53, January, 1912, "Persia, Russia, and Shuster."

[4] For England's part in Moroccan question, see J. Holland Rose, "The Origins of the War," chap. IV, "Morocco"; Perseus, "Morocco and Europe: The Task of Sir Edward Grey," *Fortnightly Review*, 85:609-624, April, 1906.

in case of hostility, as was so effectively done at the opening of the great war.

This realignment of British policy produced two outstanding conditions in world politics: the isolation of Germany, and the supremacy of Japan in the East. Germany was not in favour of having Japan dominate Manchuria and Korea and occupy the premier commercial position on the Asiatic mainland, but she was too busily engaged to oppose the Entente Powers in Europe to make any effective resistance against Japan's encroachment in China. The only nation that was in a position to assist China to preserve her autonomy against foreign aggression was the United States. The United States has political reasons and commercial interests as well as a sense of moral obligation which should lead her to help China preserve her national integrity. The Hay " open door " doctrine, promoted by the American Government and agreed to by other nations, provided equality of commercial privileges in, and the preservation of the political independence and territorial integrity of China. By virtue of its origin and of the leadership of John Hay, the United States was made an unofficial sponsor for this doctrine, which is still in existence. Politically, domination of China by one power means the lessening of American influence and prestige in the Far East, and a direct menace to the American insular possessions. Commercially, the monopoly of the Chinese market, or of the market of one province, as in the case of Manchuria, signifies the driving out of American trade in the monopolized territory. There were ample reasons for the United States to propose to neutralize the Manchurian railways. But the immediate occasion that enabled Secretary Knox to make the neutralization proposal was a concession to build the Chinchow-Aigun railway given by the Chinese Government to an American concern. Thus by neutralizing all railways in Manchuria, America had its share of monopoly to give up.

The proposal provided " to take the railroads of Manchuria out of Eastern politics and place them under an economic and impartial administration by vesting in China the ownership of its railroads; the funds for that purpose to be furnished by the nationals of such interested powers as might be willing to participate and who are pledged to the policy of the open door and equal opportunity, the powers participating to operate the railway system during the period of the loan and enjoy the usual preference in supplying materials. . . . The advantages of such a plan are obvious. It would insure unimpaired Chinese sovereignty, the commercial and industrial development of the Manchurian provinces, and furnish a substantial reason for the solution of the problems of fiscal and monetary reforms which are now receiving such earnest attention of the Chinese Government. It would afford an opportunity for both Russia and Japan to shift their onerous duties, responsibilities and expenses in connection with these railways to the shoulders of the combined powers, including themselves. Such a policy, moreover, would effect a complete commercial neutralization of Manchuria, and in so doing make a large contribution to the peace of the world by converting provinces of Manchuria into an immense commercial neutral zone." [5]

On November 6, 1909, Secretary Knox sent a formal note to the British Government, asking British coöperation in the American proposal. On November 25th, Sir Edward Grey sent his reply, expressing the approval of his government of the principle involved in the plan, without, however, committing itself to any definite agreement. Secretary Knox presented his proposal simultaneously to Russia and Japan on December 18, 1909. There was a general cry of " confiscation " in both countries, despite the fact that the plan provided a legitimate compensation for their Manchurian railroads properly and impartially appraised. Their charge of " confiscation " is ironically amusing when we

[5] From a statement given to the press by the State Department, Washington, January 6, 1916.

recall that their titles to the Manchurian railroads were based on nothing short of their own confiscation of Chinese property.

Russia rejected the plan on January 22, 1910, and Japan on February 24, 1910. Great Britain and France stood by the decision of their respective allies—Japan and Russia. The American public, instead of supporting its statesman in his attempt to give a legitimate protection to American interests abroad, condemned the Knox policy in China and also in Central America as " dollar diplomacy." [*]

3. "DOLLAR DIPLOMACY"

This " dollar diplomacy " was soon changed with the coming in of the Democratic administration in 1913, and the American Far Eastern policy was correspondingly weakened. The new government of the Chinese Republic, after the revolution of 1911–12, was in dire need of funds, and decided to borrow money from the bankers of the United States, Great Britain, France, Germany, Japan, and Russia. The terms of this loan—commonly known as the " six-power loan "—were none too agreeable to the Chinese. They provided how the money thus borrowed should be spent, and what measures the creditor nations should take to collect the money in case

[*] See Fish, " American Diplomacy," p. 459; F. C. Howe, " Dollar Diplomacy," *Annals of American Political and Social Science*, 68: 312–320, November, 1916.

China failed to meet her part of the agreement as provided in the terms. The Chinese were afraid that such an arrangement might Egyptianize their country; yet they had no alternative. Money they must have to pay the soldiers and to meet foreign and domestic obligations incidental to the revolution. The loan nations were withholding recognition of the Republic of China to press their terms on the newly born republic.

President Wilson promptly reversed the policy of the previous administration, and led the way, on March 18, 1913, to the recognition of the new Republic of China. He withdrew government support of the " six-power loan," declaring that " the conditions of the loan seem to us to touch very nearly the administrative independence of China itself, and this administration does not feel that it ought, even by implication, to be a party to those conditions." As a result, the American bankers withdrew from the syndicate. It must be remembered that doing business in an unstable country like China is not like carrying on a commercial transaction in the United States. Foreign capital is insecure in a country where bandit raids and political revolutions are of common occurrence, unless it be backed by its government.[1]   Here is where the

_____
[1] See Tyler Dennett, " The Road to Peace, via China," *Outlook*, 117: 168-169, October 3, 1917.

principle of "trade follows the flag" comes in. Commercial exploitation is usually the pioneer of political exploitation. There is no question that this act of President Wilson is just and statesman-like, and in line with the American traditional foreign policy. It invoked, as it should have done, universal approval both at home and abroad.[8] But from the Chinese point of view, the withdrawal of American bankers from the "six-power loan" was a disappointment.

The United States has always stood for justice and fair play to China, and has more than once thrown its weight toward the preservation of the administrative and territorial integrity of that tottering nation. Had the American bankers stayed in the group, and been supported by the American Government, it would have made the United States a participant in foreign interests in China; and the State Department at Washington would have an opportunity to wield a moral lever in urging moderation on the part of other creditor nations, as was done by John Hay in the Boxer settlement. But, as it was, the United States became a disinterested power —an outsider with respect to the international struggle for zones of influence in China—leav-

[8] See "Recognition at Last," *Independent*, 74: 1009–1010, May 8, 1913; "U. S. Recognizes China," *Outlook*, 104: 41, May 10, 1913.

ing the infant republic to its own fate amid a
pack of wolfish nations. The Sherman anti-
trust law would be an asset in the development
of world trade, should it be made an international commercial code. But it is a fatal mistake to apply this restriction to American foreign trade alone, while other foreign capital is
not only protected but supported and subsidized
by interested governments, and foreign invest-
ors are even sometimes encouraged to resort to
illegitimate business methods for the capture of
foreign markets.[9] The failure of American
statesmen to appreciate this fact has caused
American trade and investment in China to decline, whereas its powerful competitor, Japanese
trade, has increased by leaps and bounds, and
is still so increasing.

In 1914 China decided to build a naval base
on the coast of Fukien. British, American, and
Japanese firms were bidding against one another to supply the material. Finally the Bethlehem Steel Corporation succeeded in getting
the contract for the work. Japan immediately
made representations to the State Department
through Ambassador Chinda that the entrench-
ment of American interest in Fukien Province,
which is in the Japanese " sphere," and the

[9] For Japanese trade methods in China, see Tong, " American Money and Japanese Brains in China," *Review of Reviews,* 53 : 452–455, April, 1916; *idem* in *Harper's Weekly,*
62 : 298–299, March, 1916.

building of a naval base with American money on Chinese coast right opposite to Formosa would be an " unfriendly act." Secretary Bryan promptly sent a cablegram to Minister Reinsch at Peking to inform the Chinese Government that the United States would not support the American interest. Thus American capital, instead of receiving subsidies and protection from its home government, as does Japanese capital, was hampered by American political leaders.

4. The Twenty-one Demands

The greatest diplomatic struggle that China has had since the Boxer settlement in 1900–01 was with Japan in 1915 over what was known as the Twenty-one Demands, made upon China by Japan.[10] These demands embody serious encroachments of Chinese rights, such as that the Chinese Government must employ influential Japanese as advisers in political, financial, and military affairs; that the policing of important places in China must be jointly administered by Japanese and Chinese; that China must purchase from Japan fifty per cent. or more of its munitions of war, and that Japanese experts must be employed in the arsenals. There is no

[10] Concerning Japan's control of public opinion in connection with the Twenty-one Demands, see Part II, Chapter III, § III.

question but that had China conceded to these demands *in toto,* the Eastern Republic would be a dependency of Japan to-day.

The demands were first presented to the Chinese Government on January 18, 1915, when representatives of several important news services and papers were absent from Peking in Japan. Japan had intended to intimidate China into concession of these demands in secret. When the news began to leak out, Japan, through her diplomatic representatives abroad, denied the demands; when denial was no longer possible, she gave out a false series of demands for publication abroad.[11] When, however, the real demands began to come to light from the Chinese official source, not only the Chinese themselves, but the foreigners in China were alarmed and indignant. The British commercial interests in China made vigorous representations to their home government for protest against Japan's demands. American missionaries in China sent a memorial to President Wilson asking for American mediation in the crisis.[12]

There was a general uproar of indignation in the House of Commons when the news of the demands reached London. But the British Gov-

[11] Eleven articles published in the London *Times,* as coming from the Japanese Embassy at London, quoted by Millard, "Our Eastern Question," pp. 146–147.
[12] See the text of the memorial, Part III, S.

ernment was in no position to oppose Japan. There was only one nation that was in a position to make an effective resistance to the Japanese aggression in China, and that nation was the United States. But all the American Government did was to make an inquiry of Japan as to what she was doing in China, basing the right of inquiry on the American-Japanese agreement of 1908 regarding China: " Should any event occur threatening the *status quo* . . . or the principle of equal opportunity . . . it remains for the two governments to communicate with each other in order to arrive at an understanding as to what measures they may consider it useful to take." [12]

Publicity compelled Japan to modify somewhat the original demands. On April 26, 1915, the Japanese minister at Peking presented revised demands in twenty-four articles. On May 7th Japan delivered to the Chinese Government an ultimatum providing that unless a satisfactory reply be given to the demands by six o'clock on the ninth day of May, " the Imperial Japanese Government will take such steps as they may deem necessary." The Chinese Government waited as long as it could, hoping for foreign aid to relieve the pressure. But none came. After the agreements had been made and the demands granted, the American Gov-

[12] See full text of the agreement, Part III, L.

ernment notified the Chinese Government, on May 16, 1915, to the effect that " it cannot recognize any agreement or undertaking which has been entered into, or which may be entered into between the governments of China and Japan impairing the treaty rights of the United States and its citizens in China, the political or territorial integrity of the Republic of China, or the international policy, commonly known as the open door policy." [14] An identical note was sent to the Japanese Government.

5. CHINA AND THE EUROPEAN WAR

After the United States severed its diplomatic relations with Germany, February 3, 1917, President Wilson sent a note to China advising her to follow the American example. It was largely through the influence of Dr. Paul S. Reinsch, the American minister at Peking, in combination with the Chinese liberals, that China was persuaded to follow the American lead and was brought into the ranks of the Allies.[15]

During the short period of the attempted restoration of the monarchy by Chang Hsun and

[14] See Part III, R.
[15] For a full account of China's entering the war and the reasons for it, see Stanley K. Hornbeck, " Tricks That are Vain—in Chinese Politics," *Review of Reviews,* 56 : 172–175, August, 1917; " China's Part in the War," the *Illustrated London News,* 151 : 249, September, 1917.

Kang Yu Wei,[16] in the summer of 1917, when China was on the verge of shipwreck, Secretary Lansing sent a sympathetic note to the Chinese Government through Minister Reinsch, expressing regret for the dissensions in China, and the hope that stable government would be established, and extending America's sincere good wishes. This note was severely criticized by the Japanese press as an infringement of Japan's paramount interest in China. Japan does not give any direct advices to Mexico, the Nipponese press argued, and why should the United States attempt to exercise any influence over China, the country over which Japan has as much tutelage as the United States has over Mexico? Any advice to be given China by the United States, the Japanese suggested, ought to have been given through Japan.[17] This haughty attitude of Japan brought forth some sharp retorts on the part of the American press. Said the New York *Morning Telegraph:* " Why should the United States of America, the most powerfull democracy in the world, consult the Japanese monarchy, recently delivered, in part, from

[16] See " China Foils a Royalist Coup," New York *Times, Current History,* 6, pt. 2: 259–260, August, 1917; Carl Crow, " Chang, the Unchanging," *Sunset Magazine,* 39: 12–13, August, 1917.

[17] The comparison of the Japanese position in China with the American position in Mexico is a hobby of the Japanese publicists: see statement by K. K. Kawakami, quoted by Millard in " Our Eastern Question," p. 297.

paganism before admonishing the Chinese people? . . . To have advised with Japan would
have been officially acknowledging the para-
mountcy of Japan in that section of the world.
This we will never do."

It will be of particular interest to the American reader to know that Japan did her best to
keep China out of the war, feeling that Japanese
interests would be better served if China were
not a belligerent.   Japan preferred to deal with
China herself; she did not care to have China
given a voice at the Peace table.   Late in 1915,
on the advice of the European Allies, China
practically completed plans for entering the
war.   On that occasion, Viscount Ishii, then
Japanese Minister of Foreign Affairs, said to the
European Ambassadors at Tokyo: "Japan could
not view without apprehension the moral awakening of 400,000,000 Chinese which would result from their entering the war."   Japan's opposition was so definite and so potent that the
Chinese plan of entering the war was blocked.
Not until March, 1917, after obtaining secret
promises from the European Allies that they
would support Japan's claims at the Peace table
and that Japan would not be interfered with in
carrying out her program in China, and when it
became clear that Japan was not able to checkmate the combined efforts of the European
Allies and the United States to bring China into

the war on the side of the, Allies, Japan withdrew her objection.[18] The Chinese Government, after formally declaring war upon Germany, offered to send 100,000 troops to Europe to help the Allies; but Japan, unwilling to have China take so active a part, vetoed the plan.

[18] See official dispatch from M. Krupensky, former Russian Ambassador at Tokyo, to Minister of Foreign Affairs in Petrograd, February 8, 1917, cited in *The Secret Treaties and Understandings,* published by the Russian Revolutionary Government.

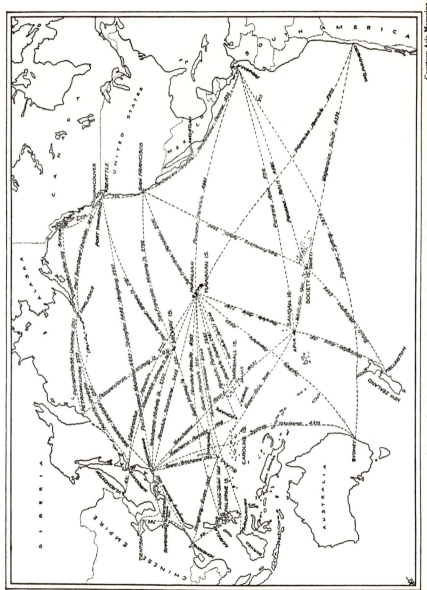

IV

THE LANSING-ISHII AGREEMENT

1. The Diplomatic Procedure

A LATE development of the American Oriental policy is the Lansing-Ishii agreement of November 2, 1917, based on notes exchanged between Secretary of State Lansing and Ambassador Ishii, the head of the Japanese War Mission which visited the United States. The obvious purpose of this mission, as was announced by the Japanese Government, was to follow the example of the English, French, and Italian War Missions to America in furthering the better understanding between America and Japan, and the closer cooperation in the war against the "Common Enemy."[1] But a closer investigation of the accomplishments of this mission in America reveals something deeper than these obvious reasons. The Japanese War Mission, like all

[1] See addresses of Ambassador Kikujiro Ishii at various places in America, New York *Times, Current History,* VI: 429–430, September, 1917; *ibid.,* VII: 50–52, October, 1917.

other Japanese undertakings, had an ulterior motive.

There are three outstanding issues between the United States and Japan that must be settled sooner or later. They are the " open door " question in China, the question of immigration, and the question of Japanese citizenship in America. The first of these hinders commercial development and political expansion of Japan, and the other two are an open insult to the honour and integrity of Japan,—at least, the Japanese think so. The purpose of this mission was to reach a satisfactory agreement concerning the first of these three issues,—blindly satisfactory to America and selfishly gratifying to Japan. A brief review of what the mission has accomplished unmistakably points to this conclusion.

Japan could not have selected a better man to head this mission than Viscount Ishii, whose knowledge of international etiquette, and whose rhetorical perfection in the English language are equal to that of the best in the West.[2] In his speech before the United States Senate, the Japanese ambassador inspired thunderous applause by declaring, " We of Japan took up arms against Germany because a solemn treaty was not to us a scrap of paper. We did not enter

[2] See " Japanese Mission," *Review of Reviews,* 56 : 361, October, 1917.

into this war because we had any selfish interest to promote or any ill-conceived ambition to gratify."[3] These statements are ironically amusing when we remember what Japan has done in Korea despite all her solemn treaty obligations to the Hermit Kingdom;[4] and more recently in China, ignoring not only her treaty obligations with China and other treaty powers, but breaking faith with her ally—England.[5] When Japan declared war upon Germany, August 15, 1914, Count Okuma, then Premier of Japan, telegraphed to an American magazine assuring "the people of America and of the world that Japan has no ulterior motive, no desire to secure more territory, no thought of depriving China or other peoples of anything which they now possess."[6] The sincerity of this statement was tested when, in less than a year, Japan made the well-known Twenty-one Demands upon China. Japanese statesmen stated more than once that Japan was to take Tsingtau with the intention of returning it to

[3] *Congressional Record*, vol. 55, No. 124, p. 7040, August 30, 1917.
[4] For Japan's perfidy with Korea, consult F. A. McKenzie, "The Tragedy of Korea," chapter on "Treaty-Making and Treaty-Breaking."
[5] For Japan's aggressions on China despite her treaty obligations to the contrary, consult Millard, "Our Eastern Question," chapters on "Japan's Aggressions on China."
[6] Cablegram sent to the *Independent* (New York), August 24, 1914, published in the *Independent*, August 31, 1914, vol. 79, p. 291. See Part III, M.

China.[1] All the treaties, promises, and declarations made by the Japanese statesmen concerning their policy on the Asiatic mainland have so far been mere scraps of paper. Yet this ambassador extraordinary from Japan blandly told the most august body of American lawmakers that Japan respected treaty obligations and had entered the war unselfishly.

At the public dinner given in honour of the Japanese Mission by Mayor Mitchel, in New York City, September 29, 1917, Viscount Ishii outlined the Japanese policy in China as follows:

"Circumstances for which we were in no sense responsible gave us certain rights in Chinese territory, but at no time in the past and at no time in the future do we or will we seek to take territory from China or to despoil China of her rights. We wish to be and always continue to be the sincere friend and helper of our neighbour, for we are more interested than any one else, except China, in good government there. Only we must at all times for self-protection prevent other nations from doing what we have no right to do. We not only will not seek to assail the integrity or the sovereignty of China, but will eventually be prepared to de-

[1] This promise has never been fulfilled. See Millard, "Our Eastern Question," chapter on "Japan's Seizure of Kiaochow," and Part III, S; also, *World's Work*, 35: 125–126, December, 1917; *Independent*, 79: 293, August 31, 1914.

fend and maintain the integrity and independence of China against any aggressor. . . .
The door is always open. It always has been open; it always must remain open to representatives of these vast commercial interests represented so well in this great gathering of kings of commerce. We went to China where the door was open to us as to you, and we always have realized that there nature gave us an advantage. There was no need, there is no need to close that door on you, because we welcome your fair and honest competition." [8]

Then he described what the American public had heard concerning Japanese activities in China as false rumours manufactured by the German propagandists in China and America to estrange the friendship between the United States and Japan. These public declarations of the Japanese ambassador were cheered by more than a thousand public men; they were flashed all over the country, and were hailed everywhere by the press as the keynote of the Japanese Monroe Doctrine based on "broad and altruistic principles." [9] "The statement should relieve the hyper-sensitive alarm over the purpose of Japan in the East," said Ex-President

[8] See "Japan's New Pledge Regarding China," New York Times, Current History, VII: 356–357, November, 1917.
[9] See "The Japanese Mission," Independent, 92: 79, October 13, 1917; "Japan, America, and the East," Outlook, 117: 200, October 10, 1917.

Taft in his telegram to the United Press on October 1st, commenting on the Ishii declaration. " It manifested a spirit of friendship to the United States and a pledge to maintain and preserve China from spoliation which was most reassuring." [10]

On November 2,·1917, formal notes were exchanged between Secretary Lansing and Ambassador Ishii. The agreement in main provides: (1) that the United States recognizes Japan's special interests in China based on territorial propinquity; (2) that both the United States and Japan recognize the principle of " open door " and integrity of China." Besides these formal agreements contained in the note, "A complete and satisfactory understanding upon the matter of naval coöperation in the Pacific for the purpose of attaining the common object against Germany and her allies has been reached between the representatives of the imperial Japanese navy who are attached to the special mission of Japan and the representatives of the United States navy." [12]

2. RECEPTION OF THE AGREEMENT

With the exception of a few publicists who

[10] Press dispatches from New York, October 1, 1917.
[11] See Part III, T.
[12] From the official statement given to the press by the State Department, November 6, 1917.

know the Eastern politics and are familiar with the methods of Japanese diplomacy,[13] this new agreement between the United States and Japan received the most favourable comment in the press and from the public men in America.[14] Apparently it cleared away the threatening cloud on the Eastern horizon; put an end to the yellow peril; and solved the perplexing Eastern question, together with its corollary—the question of the mastery of the Pacific.   Even louder praises came from Japan.   From the Japanese publicity channels and officially manipulated press, we heard that the news of the agreement was heralded throughout the Empire as a new bond of the time-honoured friendship between America and Japan; that in the Japanese mind this new agreement signalized the permanent peace in the Pacific basin, and expressed the cordial friendship of America and Japan toward China in a genuine spirit of helpfulness.

Amid all these tumults of applause, both in America and Japan, the Associated Press received the following cablegram from its Peking agent, dated October 26th, which dispatch, owing to the supreme prestige of Japan at that

[13] See " The Proper Interpretation of the Agreement," *Nation*, 105: 563–565, November 22, 1917, by Herald Monk Vinacke.

[14] See " Monroe and Ishii Doctrine," *Independent*, 92: 309, November 17, 1917; for press editorials, see *Literary Digest*, November 17, 1917, vol. 55: pp. 15–16.

moment, received practically no publicity in the American press:

"The Japanese are exerting every effort, officially and unofficially, to close the Chinese arms monopoly contract, carrying control of the Nanking iron deposits and the employment of Japanese military advisers and a director of the new arsenal at Nanking. It is asserted by the Japanese that they are extending credit, and not making a loan, and consequently that they are not violating the six Powers' exclusive rights to make political loans.

"This view is not shared by the French and the English and a large section of the Chinese press, as well as diplomatic circles, which unite in denouncing the deal as a revival of the most objectionable feature in Japan's demands presented to China in May, 1915, known as 'Group Five.' The principal provisions of those demands, which were twenty-one in number, concerned the appointment of Japanese military and political advisers for China and Japanese supervision over the manufacture or purchase by China of munitions of war.

"Minister Reinsch has advised the Foreign Office that China has invariably taken the position that it would hold the remainder of the iron deposits for national use whenever Americans have sought development rights, and that consequently the United States now would insist that American interests be given consideration in the Chinese iron industry. The ministers of several other countries have taken the same position." [15]

To the average American mind it is quite incredible that Japan should assure the United States, through her special mission, of her intention of preserving China's integrity and the principle of equal opportunities in the East, and at the same time secretly attempt to undermine these very principles. [16] Still more incredible is the Chinese protest against the friendly and altruistic intentions of Japan that the Island Empire " not only will not seek to assail the integrity or the sovereignty of China, but will eventually be prepared to defend and maintain the integrity and independence of China against any aggressor." The Lansing-Ishii agreement is bitterly resented by the Chinese." [17] It was

[15] *World's Work* (New York), 35: 125–126, December, 1917. This attempt of Japan has resulted in the appointment of Baron Yoshiro Sakatani as the Japanese Financial Adviser to the Chinese Government, and in the conclusion of the new Sino-Japanese Military Agreement (Part III, U) of March 19, 1918; see Hollington K. Tong, " What Japan Really Wants of China," *Millard's Review* (Shanghai), IV: 264–267, April 20, 1918; " Japan Completing Financial Control of China," *ibid.*, IV: 457–459, May 25, 1918.

[16] See Frederick Moore, " The Japanese Menace to China," *World's Work*, 35: 196–207, December, 1917.

[17] At a mass meeting of Chinese students in Tokyo, Japan, resolutions were adopted condemning the declarations of Viscount Ishii in America as hypocritical professions to conceal the real designs of Japan toward China,—*New Korea* (San Francisco), p. 3, November 8, 1917.

criticized not only by the press of the Eastern republic, but by the government officials as well. Formal representations were made by the Chinese Government both at Tokyo and at Washington to the effect that "the Chinese Government will not allow itself to be bound by any agreement entered into by other nations," that China is an independent nation, and ought not to be the subject of negotiations between foreign countries.[18] China is, indeed, surprised "that America, of all countries, should have taken this step and lent herself, however unwillingly, to Japanese imperial schemes," as the *Peking Gazette* puts it.[19]

This protest from China is not inspired altogether by a sensitive self-respect or an injured pride from the fact that sovereign China is about to be "protected" by Japan,—the construction put upon Chinese expressions by many journals in America. Rather it is due to the Chinese fear of Japan and her conviction that Japanese designs in China are contrary to the public declarations of the Nipponese statesmen. Dr. Ng. Poon Chew, the eminent Chinese scholar and publicist, gives expression to the enlightened Chinese sentiment regarding the new pact as follows: "During Japan's war with Russia, twelve years ago, Japan declared to the

[18] Press dispatches from Washington, November 10, 1917.
[19] Quoted in *Literary Digest,* p. 8, November 24, 1917.

world that the motives which impelled her to take arms against Russia were to drive Russia from Manchuria and restore Manchuria to its rightful owner, China. Twelve years have elapsed since the conclusion of that war. What part of Manchuria has Japan restored to China? Not only none, but to-day Japan occupies a larger sphere of Manchuria than Russia ever occupied. Japan has done everything to hinder, obstruct, and frustrate China's plans to develop Manchuria under Chinese Government auspices. Japan is the Prussia of Asia. She stands to-day for the very principles against which the Allied nations are fighting. If Japan to-day is allowed a free hand to dispose of China the war now being fought at such a terrible cost in Europe must be fought all over in Asia. It is not to the interest of the world to permit Japan to have a free hand in China." [20]

3. Effect on Japanese Attitude

" Is there any substantial reason for the Chinese distrust of Japanese policy in China? " the American reader may ask. Had the United States Government given China the same pledge that Japan has given in the recent American-Japanese pact, China would be elated, for it has been the history of commercial development in

[20] Published in the *Sacramento Bee,* quoted in the *Literary Digest,* November 24, 1917, pp. 16–17.

China of late years that whatever advantage Japan obtained from the Chinese she got through coercion, whereas American capitalists are invited to develop Chinese resources.[21] Time, the great revealer of truth, will in the future expose the hidden ambition of Japan concerning China, and her real purposes in making this new agreement with America. At present, there is only one way in which we can form a reasonably accurate opinion as to the ulterior motives of an aggressive empire, that is to deduce current policies from existing facts in the light of past experience. What in Japanese diplomacy of the recent past has been indicative of the present Japanese Asiatic policy? What part should the United States take in the shaping of events in the Far East? Upon the correct analysis and proper solution of this problem hinges the future peace in the Pacific basin and the welfare of one-fourth of the world's population. If the problem be correctly solved, and the situation wisely handled, the Pacific Ocean in the future will be a basin of cultural and commercial activities; the United States will hold her political prestige and commercial advantages in the East; the oldest civilization in the world will be preserved, and

[21] See Minister Wellington Koo's speech at a meeting of U. S. Chamber of Commerce, New York *Times,* February 10, 1916.

China will in time take her place among the
powers of the world. If, on the other hand,
the Asiatic question is left to a hit-or-miss policy
with a lax and indifferent attitude, Asia will
ultimately be consolidated under Japanese
domination. Asia, with great natural resources
and limitless man-power, dominated by an
aggressive empire, European or Asiatic, is a
menace to the world's peace, and a direct threat
to the welfare of the United States.

The habitable area of the earth is limited, and
China is the last remaining unprotected El
Dorado in the world. There are two elements
that an ambitious nation must have in order to
be great,—great in the material sense: wealth
and man-power. China has both; she has
abundant natural resources to be developed, and
four hundred million sturdy people to be
secured for use in war or peace. But China is
no nation; she is a collection of four hundred
million individuals. Common ties of political
aspiration, economic interdependence, and
social obligation are almost utterly lacking.
Nationalism in the modern sense of the word is
an unknown quantity to the masses of China.
European nations took advantage of this, and
through one pretext after another obtained
leases, concessions, and spheres of influence in
China until the autonomy of that ancient nation
became only a nominal term.

Japan, the infant prodigy of the East, crowded for space for her ever-increasing population,[22] and with an insatiable desire to become a first class power among the family of nations, has a vision of political and commercial expansion on the mainland of Asia. *Consolidation of Asia under Japanese domination* is the soul of Japanese foreign policy, and has been so ever since Japan became a modern nation.[23] In the first blocking out of her program she proposed to annex Korea within forty-nine years, but this has been accomplished in twenty-six.[24] Now the same process is being repeated in China. Already Japan dominates Manchuria, Inner Mongolia, Fukien, Shantung and Liaotung.[25] The same policy—the policy of opportunism—that was used so effectively in undermining the Korean Government is in full operation in China now, and the same Japanese minister, Count Gonsuke Hayashi, who was instrumental in destroying Korea, is now the Japanese minister at Peking. The open door principle is practically destroyed,

---

[22] Annual increase of population in Japan proper is estimated at 600,000; see W. E. Weyl, "Japan's Menacing Birth-rate," *Asia*, 18: 129-133, February, 1918.

[23] See Walter E. Weyl, "Japan's Diplomacy of Necessity," *Asia*, XVII: 593-595, October, 1917.

[24] See McKenzie, "The Tragedy of Korea"; Park, "The Tragic History of Korea," Chinese and Korean editions.

[25] See Millard, "The Far Eastern Question," "Our Eastern Question"; J. W. Jenks, "Japan's Acts in China," *World's Work*, 33: 312-328, January, 1917.

for in the territories controlled by the Japanese, the door is open only to Japanese trade.[26]

With money borrowed from the British capitalists, the Japanese built the South Manchurian Railway and shut off British trade. British financiers have now come to realize that every time they lend a pound to the Japanese, that money is used in the East to kill the British trade; and to-day the Japanese cannot borrow a single shilling in the London markets. Hence they turn to the United States.[27] Money they must have to develop all the mining and railroad concessions wrenched from China. In 1916, Baron Shibusawa, the Japanese Morgan and the semi-official spokesman of the government, came to the United States to arrange a huge loan with the bankers of New York. His mission was a failure. But had he been successful and had he borrowed enough money from American capitalists, it is very probable that the Japanese could have succeeded in closing all the doors of China to the rest of the world, as they have done in Manchuria.

It has been stated time and again that Japan entered the European War with the unselfish

---

[26] See O. K. Davis, "Whose Open Door?" *Everybody's,* 36: 34–46, January, 1917.
[27] See H. K. Tong, "American Money and Japanese Brains," *Review of Reviews,* 53: 452–455, April, 1916; "Japan, China, and American Money," *Harper's Weekly,* 62: 298–299, March 26, 1916.

motive of fulfilling her treaty obligation to her ally—England. That may or may not be true. But the fact is that Japan is the only nation that has profited by this war. It seems likely that Japan will occupy all the territories formerly held by Germany in the Far East and more. Commercially, she is enjoying an unprecedented prosperity. She has replaced all the German and Austrian, and a part of the Allies' trade in the East. Since the war began, Japan's sales to the Philippines, Straights Settlements, British India, Australia, and Spain have more than doubled. Sales to Russia are more than twelve times what they were;[28] Egypt has changed from a modest customer requiring less than a half million dollars' worth of goods yearly to a fairly important one buying more than five times that amount. The United States bought in 1916 a hundred million dollars' worth more than in 1913. "Japan is enjoying the novel experience of engaging in a war which has brought great prosperity, with no increase in taxes, no issues of bonds, and with no loss to army and navy."[29]

[28] This was true up to the time of the overthrow of the Kerensky government, November, 1917. Since then the trade relations between Japan and Russia have been uncertain because of the unstable condition of Russia.

[29] Carl Crow, "Get-Rich-Quick Japan," *Sunset Magazine*, 39 : 32–33, December, 1917. Also see G. L. Harding, "Japan's Part in the War," New York *Times, Current History*, VI : 528–531, September, 1917.

The Lansing-Ishii agreement, regardless of what the American people may think of it, is, in the opinion of Japanese and Chinese, a decided victory for Japan and a corresponding defeat for America.[20] Recognition of sovereignty within sovereignty is contradiction of terms. No matter what the intention of the American statesmen in recognizing Japan's special interests in China, the Japanese purpose in making this agreement is to blindfold America as to their ever-increasing activities in China, and to make America ignore China's appeal against the Japanese aggression.

[20] For full discussion of this topic, see the present writer's "China's Distrust of Japan," *Asia*, XVIII: 225–226, March, 1918.

V

PRESENT POLICIES AND OPPORTUNITIES

1. JAPANESE PLANS AND AMBITIONS

THE astute statesmen of Japan realize the solidarity of public opinion in the West. Hence their advance on the Asiatic mainland has been very cautious. As long as they get what they want piecemeal, it will not attract Western attention, nor will any single loss be great enough to arouse the Chinese to a fighting spirit. Through this policy—the policy of the small snake with the big toad—Japan has swollen her sphere of influence during the last ten years to the largest in the mainland of Asia. If this policy is permitted to proceed unchecked, Japan will ultimately succeed in absorbing the entire continent of Asia with its vast natural resources and limitless manpower. Then no longer could the British colonies discriminate against Japanese immigrants;[1] no longer could California pass an alien land law; no longer could the United States Government assert the principles of Monroe Doctrine that the Western Hemisphere is closed to imperial colonization. *Banzai* and

[1] See Harry C. Douglas, "What May Happen in the Pacific," *Review of Reviews*, 55 : 394–398, April, 1917.

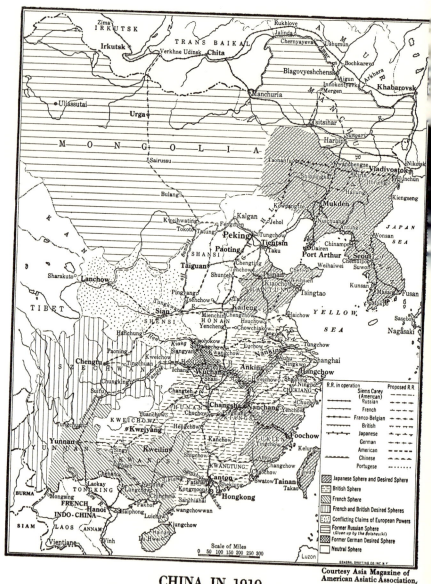

CHINA IN 1919

SHOWING RAILWAYS AND SPHERES OF INFLUENCE

The Spheres Vary Broadly from the British Centres of Economic Influence Based on Years of Developed Commerce and Investment to the Japanese, Where Political Authority Advances Hand in Hand With Economic Advantage. A Crucial Test of the League of Nations Be Its Ability or Failure to End Them by Substituting a Workable Plan of International Cooperation.

Dai Nippon will be far more dangerous and for-midable than *Kultur* and *Weltpolitik*. With these outstanding facts and tendencies in view, what should be the correct Oriental policy of the United States?

Japan will regard—outwardly, at least—the wishes of the United States as long as the United States is superior in resources and man-power. But Japan will not remain inferior to the United States in these two elements essen-tial to a nation's greatness, if her present policy is carried out successfully. She patiently fore-bore the insolence of China during the early years of the Meiji Era, only saying to herself, "We will come back at China when we are ready and able." She redeemed this pledge to herself in 1894. After the Chino-Japanese War, Russia, Germany, and France drove her out of Liaotung Peninsula. She acquiesced in what she deemed to be the humiliating terms of these three powers, but with the anticipation of com-ing back at them in the future. Come back she did in 1904 and 1914, to Russia and Germany respectively. The dates 1924 and 1934 are open, and Japan has a few more issues to settle with foreign nations—especially with the United States—and a few more self-made pledges to redeem. Here it might be well to remember the significant statement of Baron Kato, Min-ister for Foreign Affairs, in the Japanese Diet on January 21, 1915, on the pending California Alien Land Law question: "The Imperial Government has found the replies of the American Government not at all satisfactory and recognizes the necessity of elaborating other plans for the solution of the pending question. As regards the nature of these plans, the time to report them has not, to our regret, arrived."[1]

The American diplomacy in the Far East has been a "diplomacy *de luxe*," as a Japanese publicist once described it. American statesmen piously believe in the open door and integrity of China, but the idea of fighting for these ideals has never entered their minds. They have honourable intentions in regard to their foreign policy and judge the intentions of the Japanese statesmen by their own. The American lack of preparation, both military and psychological, to fight for what she believes in concerning China gave Japan freedom of action in the East, and the self-deceiving good intention of American diplomacy furnished an ample opportunity for Japan to hoodwink the United States. Count Okuma is a powerful imperialist; he believes in anything but fairness and non-aggression toward China. Yet he is the president of the Japan Peace Society that manufactures peace propaganda, not for home con-

[1] Quoted by Millard in "Our Eastern Question," pp. 223-224.

sumption, but for export purposes—especially to the United States. General Terauchi, the premier of Japan, is an out-and-out militarist, yet he sends out for American consumption doctrines of peace and democracy as the "national sentiment of the Japanese people." At present, Japan has no more intention of making an aggressive war upon the United States than she has of making an aggressive war on Great Britain. But she wants to create in America an impression that Japan is a formidable nation with matchless fighting machines, that the United States must let her alone and stay out of her way in Asia. So far Japan has succeeded admirably in all her diplomatic game of bluff with the United States.

The lax and indifferent Oriental policy of the American Government and the failure to understand the nature of Japanese diplomacy have caused the decrease of American trade and prestige in the East. American exports to China fell in ten years (1905–1915) from about twenty-eight per cent. of China's total imports to less than eight per cent.[2] The Japanese in China are working insidiously to undermine American influence and prestige. In exerting their pressure to cancel the Chinchow-Aigun railway concession, a concession given to the Bethlehem Steel Corporation, the Japanese

[2] Millard, "Our Eastern Question," p. 356.

minister at Peking used these significant words in his note to the Chinese Government, January 31, 1910: " Before the Chinese Government determines anything, the consent of my government must first be obtained." [*]   While Minister Reinsch was wielding his influence to induce China to follow the example of the United States in breaking off relations with Germany in the spring of 1917, Japanese agents in China secretly combined with the German and Austrian propagandists to block the move.   When finally the Chinese liberals won over the reactionaries in breaking off the diplomatic relation with Germany, then both official Tokyo and the Japanese press sent to America and Europe dispatches containing loud praises of the Chinese decision.

This insidious attempt of the Japanese to undermine American influence is prevalent wherever the interests of the two nations come into contact.   Although it has been denied by the Japanese Government and the press, and the State Department is reticent on the Japanese part of the intrigue in the alleged German-Japanese-Mexican alliance to invade the United States, presumably because the officials at Washington do not wish to complicate matters any more than necessary concerning an ally of

[*]Note sent to Wai Wu-Pu.   See full text of the note, Millard, *ibid.,* p. 17.

the United States in the world war, there were
enough evidences in the intercepted note of the
German Foreign Minister, Alfred Zimmermann,
to the German Minister, von Eckhardt, at Mexico City, and in the information which leaked
out through non-official channels at Washington
that Japan was inclined to take sides with Germany in the attempt to arouse Mexico against
the United States, if the occasion were opportune and the methods expedient.[5]

2. AMERICAN DUTIES AND OPPORTUNITIES

Now that the European War is over, there is
likely to be a realignment of world politics, and

[5] The Zimmermann note was dated, January 19, 1917, and
was given to the press by the State Department, February
28, 1917. An interesting side-light has been shed on the "pro-
Ally" attitude of Japan during the war by Hon. Alvan T.
Fuller of Massachusetts, in his speech in Congress, March
3, 1919:
"My trip across the water was uneventful. I found among
my fellow passengers a most delightful person, who was no
other than M. Delanney, the French ambassador to Japan. I
took occasion to ask the ambassador, if, as a result of his
observation, the Japanese were sincerely pro-Ally. To this
inquiry the ambassador replied very definitely, 'No, sir,' and
inquired, 'Who in the world thought they were sincerely
pro-Ally?'
"Ambassador Delanney stated to me that the Japanese
intended to support Germany, but after the commission
visited here and saw how whole-heartedly we were going into
the war they were afraid to do so. Ambassador Delanney
stated that he sailed from Japan to Vancouver, and when the
party arrived and learned the news that Austria had sur-
rendered the Japanese members of the party were visibly
disappointed. He likened the emperor and the military caste
of Japan to that of Germany. He said their methods and
ideas and ideals were those of Germany" (*Congressional
Record,* Vol. 57, No. 86, p. 5465, March 15, 1919, 65th Congress, 3rd Session).

the United States may adopt a new Oriental policy befitting its rights and obligations. The Anglo-Japanese alliance has served its purpose, and England and Japan are only nominal allies. Already there are signs in both countries of mutual distrust.[6] British resentment of the Japanese encroachment upon their interests in the East, and the secret attempts of the Japanese to stir the Hindus against the British rule are the straws which indicate the undercurrent that drift the two allied nations apart.[7] In the proposal of Japanese intervention in Siberia, Great Britain, through her ambassador, Earl Reading, at Washington, sounded the United States on its disposition to send troops to Asia jointly with Japan, before requesting her Eastern ally to intervene. From this diplomats at Washington and elsewhere drew the inference that " Great Britain suspects Japan of an intention of staying in Siberia once she gets there.

[6] For the sentiment of Japanese publicists toward Great Britain and her policies, consult K. K. Kawakami, " Japan in World Politics " (New York), 1917.

[7] See Millard, " Our Eastern Question," chap. XIII, " Japan and Great Britain "; McKenzie, " The Tragedy of Korea," chap. XX, " Prospects for Foreign Trade." For the Japanese secret participation in Hindu revolt against the English, see the findings in the Hindu revolt plot trials in San Francisco,—press dispatches, January 19, 1918; also see the correspondence between the leaders of the Hindu Nationalists in New York, and Japanese Ambassador Aimaro Sato at Washington, intercepted by the Department of Justice, and " Isolation of Japan in World Politics," suppressed by Department of Justice, March, 1918.

Joint intervention would give handle for invoking joint withdrawal eventually."[8]

Equally as possible as the rupture of the Anglo-Japanese alliance is the formation of an Anglo-American alliance. The war aims of both England and America were practically identical and the political aspirations of the two countries have much in common. England and the United States, the two most enlightened and powerful democratic nations in the world, combined can curb the ambition of Japan—*the consolidation of Asia under Japanese domination*—thereby removing the cause for another world war, and give China political independence and economic stability. This can be done by accomplishing two things: (1) By having all the treaty powers, by some sort of a diplomatic agreement, give up the sphere doctrine and release the predatory trade privileges extorted from China. The limit of five per cent. custom duties on all imports and the exemption of foreign traders and manufacturers from internal revenue taxes have made it impossible for the native traders and manufacturers to compete with their foreign competitors and have kept the Chinese Government in perpetual insolvency.[9] When these obstacles have been eliminated,

[8] Press dispatch from Washington (*Nebraska State Journal*), March 2, 1918.
[9] See A. P. Winston, "Trade with China Fails to Increase," *Asia*, XVII:654, ff., October, 1917.

then China can establish her government on a more stable basis and begin financial reform and industrial enterprises. This will remove the cause of international rivalry in China and pave the way for the withdrawal of extraterritoriality. The Powers will thereby " enfranchise " China, as they " enfranchised " Japan in 1899. (2) By developing the Chinese natural resources through the combined capital of all Powers as Secretary Knox suggested in his plan for the neutralization of Manchurian railroads in 1909. By this plan the investing Powers will have the legitimate profit for their investment under the Chinese ownership of the enterprise. This will do away with the underhanded trade methods of rival nations and convert the Chinese field into a vast neutral zone of peaceful commerce and fair competition. It will also bring economic prosperity to the Chinese, which means a higher standard of living, enlightenment of the masses, and increase of purchasing power. If the purchasing power of China's millions be increased, she will be one of the most attractive markets in the world. Treaty Powers, including Japan, will reap the benefit in the end, although they may feel a seeming sacrifice for a time in surrendering their exclusive rights and spheres.

The United States has a unique rôle to play in this realignment of world politics and in the remaking of China. The Pacific Ocean is fast becoming the basin of political and commercial activities, and what affects one side of it is bound to affect the other. The United States cannot afford, for the safety of its own interests, to have China dominated by an aggressive and militaristic nation, European or Asiatic. The effete notion of splendid isolation is out of date, and America can no longer hold herself aloof and keep away from the entangling alliances of the old world. The world is being too closely unified for two incombatable political ideals to exist together,—imperialistic autocracy based upon militarism, and representative democracy founded on political liberty. President Wilson crystallized this idea into a political principle when he said in his message delivered at a joint session of the two houses of the Congress, April 2, 1917, . . . "The world must be made safe for democracy; its peace must be planted upon the tested foundations of political liberty. . . . We shall fight for the things which we have always carried nearest our hearts,—for democracy, for the rights of those who submit to authority to have a voice in their own governments, for the rights and liberties of small nations, for a universal domination of right by such a concert of free peoples as shall bring peace and safety to all nations and make the world itself at last free."

It is a clear enunciation of new Americanism. The United States fought for her own freedom in the Declaration of Independence. She was willing to fight for the freedom of the peoples of the Western Hemisphere in declaring the Monroe Doctrine. In the European War she fought for the freedom and democracy of the whole world. China, if unselfishly aided and wisely guided, can revive her ancient genius and develop her vast potential resources, and will eventually take her place among the powers of the world as a strong, democratic nation. Will the United States of America, true to the new principles of her political conviction, perform her mission toward China in the consummation of this noble task?

PART II

An Undercurrent Shaping the Policy : Japan's Control of Publicity

INTRODUCTION

I N the foregoing chapters we have examined briefly the development of the Oriental policy of the United States. We will now consider the subtle undercurrent that directs, in a large measure, the course of that policy.

When Germany violated Belgian neutrality and invaded France in 1914, the whole world raised its voice in indignant protest. But when Japan absorbed Korea in breach of faith and covenant to the latter Power, and in spite of her solemn declarations to the world at the beginning of the Russo-Japanese War that she was fighting Russia to safeguard the political independence and territorial integrity of Korea, the Powers of the West apparently connived at the perpetration of the crime. The national crimes that Japan committed during the course of her imperial expansion on the Asiatic mainland are not less horrible nor less excusable than those committed by Germany in Belgium and in northern France. Yet Japan has received practically no censure for what she has done in Korea and China; on the contrary, she successfully maintains her position as a worthy member of the family of the democratic nations of the world. One reason for this situation lies in her marvellously complete and skillful control of publicity, a control that enables her to manipulate easily the public opinion of the Western Powers and to mould their diplomatic policies in the Orient. A study, therefore, of the nature and extent of Japan's control of publicity will throw much light upon the diplomatic relationships of the East and the West and will result in a clearer understanding of the Oriental policy of the United States.

As early as the close of the Russo-Japanese War, before the destruction of Korean independence, Thomas F. Millard, the distinguished American publicist, wrote concerning Japanese activities in Korea:

"Nothing could display greater cleverness than the manner used by Japan through the propaganda to steadily shift her ground in regard to the main propositions involved in the settlement, while at the same time remaining carefully posed in an attitude of self-sacrifice. Something of a shock will be felt in the Western world when the mask, having served its purpose, is dropped. Meanwhile, pretense is piled upon pretense, without being able, however, to conceal the undercurrent of reality."[1]

The mask has served its purpose and is

[1] "The New Far East," p. 102.

dropped. But the act was performed so skill-fully and imperceptibly, like the transition of magic pictures on the screen, that the Western world felt no shock at all. Japan knows the publicity game and plays it well. She knows the value of honourable intentions in the public opinion of the West, and she employs every means within her power to create a most favour-able impression of herself and her aspirations in the Western world,—especially in the United States and England.

To this end, she has many agencies working constantly. They form an elaborate system of interior and exterior espionage, publicity prop-aganda, press censorship, control of the news both as to its sources and its distribution, skillful governing of the impressions made upon foreigners who visit Japan.

I

THE OFFICIAL ESPIONAGE

1. The Philosophy of the System

THERE is a wrong impression in the West that *all* the Oriental peoples are generally cunning and sly. Nothing could be further from the truth. Although the Westerner may condemn the Chinaman for his fogyism and low standard of living, he certainly may not condemn him for dishonesty. The credit system was firmly established in China long before it was known in Western Europe. There were no contractual laws in China; they were not needed, as the Chinaman's word is as good as his bond. It is a well-known fact that the Western banks in the Far East prefer Chinese cashiers to those of any other nationality. Even in Japan, the majority of the cashiers in large banks were Chinese, because of their superior commercial integrity and high code of honour, until the Japanese found out that this fact was considered a reflection on the honesty of the Japanese people before the Western public.

The Japanese themselves, before coming into

contact with the Western world, were not so
subtle as they are now. The Samurai were professional warriors. They despised wealth and
manual labour, and upheld honour and bravery.
But the swift abolition of the feudal system and
the " gulping " of Western culture,—the prod-
uct of more than five thousand years of slow
progress,—in a single generation, has made the
Japanese civilization of to-day a peculiar struc-
ture, in which the sense of proportion is almost
utterly lacking. They have copied the material
achievements of the West without absorbing the
underlying spiritual truths; they have adopted
the policy of expediency rather than principle.
The military, educational, and industrial sys-
tems of Japan are modelled after those of Germany. Their slogans, *Banzai* and *Dai Nippon*,
are other forms of " Deutschland, Deutschland,
über alles, über alles in der Welt." There is a
remarkable similarity between the Japanese spy
system and that of Germany, as was revealed at
the opening of the European War; only the
Japanese system is more elaborate, and carried
out to finer points. It is more than probable
that the aggressive Empire of Asia learned the
dishonourable but expedient trick from the
military bureaucracy of Europe, and has become
a greater master of the game.

It is needless to say that Japan reaped great
advantages from her spy system during her re-

cent wars. The Chino-Japanese War in 1894 was in many respects like the Franco-Prussian War. Every Japanese officer had a thorough knowledge of the topography of China, her resources and military strength,—all acquired through the laborious and patient work of spies long before the opening of hostilities. The same system was used in the preparation for the Russo-Japanese War. "They had military maps of every nook and corner of Korea and Manchuria; they had spies working as coolies on the Russian railroads, and in Russian ports and shipyards. . . . The collapsible boats, with which a pontoon was thrown across the Yalu, were made for that special purpose months before, when the Korean peninsula was yet to be invaded."[1] Nothing was left to chance when Japan struck the first blow, which, to the ordinary observer in the West, came like a thunderbolt from the clear sky.

In time of war, when a nation is engaged in a death struggle, espionage might be justified under the pretext of military necessity. But Japan maintains her spy system in time of peace as well as in time of war. The most curious fact about it is that so far no serious protest has been raised by *her* scholars and publicists against it. The only explanation of this strange silence is

---

[1] "The Russo-Japanese War," p. 25 (Collier and Sons, New York).

that the oft-quoted phrase of Treitschke, " der Staat ist Macht," is the ruling motto with the better thinkers of Japan, and whatever is done for the benefit of the state is justifiable. This principle was fully demonstrated in the trial and acquittal of Count Miura and his accomplices after they murdered the Korean Queen in 1895.[2] The Japanese philosophy of the state advocates selfishness and deception as motive powers that energize the world.[3] Only they appear in different manifestations in various activities of life. The forms of deception in business, for instance, are known as shrewdness; in war, they are strategy; in society, cleverness; and in relations between nations, diplomacy. But all these are only different combinations of the same element —deception.

This philosophy may find its echoes among the followers of Nietzsche and Bernhardi; but no believer in liberty and democracy can endorse it. There are a few things in human society that outrage our natural feelings, and espionage is one of them.

2. Spies in Other Lands

It is not a hasty generalization to say that

[2] See " The Far East," February, 1896, vol. I, p. 20; McKenzie, " The Tragedy of Korea," chap. VI.
[3] See Liang Ch'i-Chao, " Liberty," pp. 148–152 (Korean translation from Chinese text).

Japan has spies in practically every country on the globe. This does not mean, of course, that Japan is preparing for war on every nation in the world. But it is the Japanese way of finding out what the other people are doing. Although subtle rumours are scattered all over the United States that Japan has no use for the Philippine Islands, and that she would not occupy them under any circumstances, as they would be a burden to her;[4] yet it is an undeniable fact that the Malay Archipelagoes are honeycombed with Japanese spies.[5] In Mexico and South America there are several thousand Japanese, mostly veterans of the Russo-Japanese War. In one year, 1914, 3,675 Japanese entered Brazil.[6] According to the United States census of 1910, there were 72,157 Japanese in the United States, and 79,675 in the Hawaiian Islands. It is very probable that the number has increased considerably since. Out of this number, 123,425 were men—largely ex-soldiers.

It is merely a matter of opinion how much credence we can attribute to the newspaper reports. But it is certain that constant and repeated rumours cannot be ignored as being utterly false. They may be proofless, but they

[4] See "Why Japan does Not Want the Philippines," *Review of Reviews*, 51:494, April, 1915; also, "Philippines No Bait to Japan," *Literary Digest*, 52:1212, April 29, 1916.
[5] See S. Henschen, "What is Behind the Japanese Peril," *Forum*, 56:63–78, July, 1916.
[6] Figures taken from the *Statesmen's Year Book*, 1916.

are rarely without foundation. It was alleged that some time ago the harbour police of New York were astonished to see a Japanese aviator drop into the bay in his flying machine. He was presumably sent to map the coast defense from an aeroplane. Japanese " fishermen " were discovered near the entrance of the Panama Canal. They were trying to conduct pearl fishing expeditions by taking bearings in various sections of the bays and waters, and incidentally mapping out the forts and approaches to the canal.

" On April 28, 1916, the Mayor of Los Angeles asked the United States Government to probe the activities of Japanese in his city. Guns and supplies were found hidden in the Japanese quarters, motor trucks had been purchased, aviators were being trained, and many young Japanese had been making surveys of the coast. . . . Several months ago a Japanese was arrested in Los Angeles for drunkenness. A detailed map of the United States was found on his person. It showed landing places for aeroplanes in various parts of the country. A short time prior to this another Japanese was arrested in San Diego. He carried a complete list of all the wireless stations in the United States." [1]

Samuel G. Blythe gives an account of his knowing a Japanese nobleman in a Western hotel as a bell " hop." The films that this Japa-

[1] *Chicago Examiner,* February 4, 1917.

nese possessed showed " Mr. Togo, the boy who wore the plum-coloured suit and waited on the bell, standing on the bridge of a Japanese battleship, clad in a silk hat and a frock coat, with the insignia of a Japanese order on his breast, and between two Japanese officers, both in full naval uniform. There is a large American military post not far from the place where Togo officiated." [8]

All these reports and many others of similar nature may be discarded as fantastic and fictitious as no better than the description of the Japanese spies in Louis Joseph Vance's recent novel, " Patria." But there are two sides to every question; perhaps, indeed, this is the case with rumours as well as arguments.

One thing certain is that Japan has made persistent efforts to get a foothold on the Western Hemisphere for her military and naval purposes. In 1912, when it was known that Japanese were making secret attempts to acquire land in Magdalena Bay, under the pretext of establishing a base for Japanese fishing interests, Senator Henry Cabot Lodge, of Massachusetts, introduced a resolution in the Senate, which was adopted August 2d, declaring that " when any harbour or other place in the American continent is so situated that the occupation thereof for naval or military purposes might threaten

[8] *Saturday Evening Post*, May 22, 1915, p. 53.

the communications or the safety of the United States, the Government of the United States could not see, without grave concern, the possession of such harbour or other place by any corporation or association which has such relation to another government, not American, as to give that government traditional powers of control for naval or military purposes." Although the name Japanese was not mentioned in the resolution, that it was aimed at what Japan was trying to do was obvious. The Japanese took sufficient hint from this resolution, and gave up the attempt. It is quite clear that the American Government will not tolerate the acquisition of land in the Western Hemisphere by the Japanese for naval or military purposes, much as it is desired by the Tokyo Government.

In China the Japanese spies are not so concealed and unobtrusive as they are in the United States. A paragraph from the description of the Japanese in Manchuria by an unbiased eye-witness may be cited to illustrate the operation of the system there.

" During the Russian occupation prior to the war, the Japanese Government had sent hundreds of Japanese into the country with instructions to adopt the dress of the Chinese and domesticate themselves; and many of these persons succeeded in escaping detection after hostilities commenced, remaining to act as spies and secret agents. . . . No sooner did the Japanese armies occupy the country, and promulgate their military regulations, than these informers came out of their retirement and quickly assumed a position of importance. They pointed to the Japanese authorities Chinese who were known or suspected to sympathize with or have business relations with the Russians. It mattered little that the men thus accused might be of high standing, and the fact that a majority of them, especially officials, could not have avoided relations with the Russians. Many were executed upon the witness of these professional informers, often without even a semblance of a trial. The regulations provided that Chinese who knew of any infraction of them and failed to inform the authorities were punishable by death; while many were tortured in the attempt to force them to disclose military information." [9]

3.   ESPIONAGE IN JAPAN AND KOREA

In Japan every foreigner is watched, and everything he does and says is carefully reported and filed in the books of the government secret service office. A paragraph from the pen of the veteran correspondent, Samuel G. Blythe, after his visit to Japan, well illustrates this:

" Any man you meet may be listening for

[9] Millard, " The New Far East," p. 146.

governmental purposes to what you say or because of that natural curiosity; but in case you say anything you should not, whether the listener is a secret agent or not, he goes and reports your conversation to somebody, for that is the first duty of all Japanese—to tell what they hear. There are always some of these agents about the big hotels. They act as room-boys, as bar-boys, as waiters, and in any other capacity that will put them in contact with the guests. In the days of the Russian war the correspondents who were held in Tokyo were accustomed to relate their opinions of the Japanese in front of a certain bar, and each night complete reports of what they said were transmitted to the war office. The bar-boys were secret agents. . . . Let a man whose business is not definitely stated by him the moment he arrives go to any city in Japan, and there will be secret-service men set after him immediately. Every petty detail will be communicated to some secret head and set down painstakingly in some secret record. His trunks are likely to be opened. The boy in his room at his hotel is likely to be a spy. Every move will be watched. A man whom I know could do it told me he would get me a complete record of my comings and goings in Japan for a hundred yen. I told him it was not worth it." [10]

[10] *Saturday Evening Post,* May 22, 1915, p. 53.

The organization of the Japanese spy system in Korea is pretty nearly perfect. It is a part of the military administration in the peninsula, and is used most effectively to denationalize the ancient kingdom. A Korean is not permitted to go to Europe or America, and even within Korea the people are not allowed to travel in large groups. "Every one must be registered and is given a number, which is known to the police. Every time he leaves his village or town he must register at the police station and state fully the business he intends to transact and his destination. The policeman 'phones to this place, and if his actions are in any way at variance with his report, he is liable to arrest and mistreatment. A strict classification is kept on the basis of a man's education, influence, position, etc. As soon as a man begins to show ability or qualities of leadership he is put in class 'a,' detectives are set on his trail, and from thenceforth he becomes a marked man, hounded wherever he goes. Even children are watched or bribed for information. If a man escapes the country his number is traced, his family or relatives arrested and perchance tortured until they reveal his whereabouts. A man is likely to disappear any day and perhaps not be heard of again." [11]   Officially authorized spies are sta-

[11] J. E. Moore, "Korea's Appeal for Self-Determination," pp. 9-10.

tioned in every town and village; they force
their presence even into private household
parties. Their acts are backed by the Japanese
gendarmerie, and woe to the native who dares
to resent their intrusion! He will be charged
with treason as opposing the government authorities! The Japanese enlist as sub-spies a
large number of the worst scoundrels in the
country. These incorrigibles are paid good
salaries and in many cases given rewards for
the merit of their work; not infrequently the
well-to-do natives are blackmailed by these
spies, and the government winks at the crime.
It is not only an opportunity for petty and
venal natures to vent personal enmities and
spites, but also a chance to gather a handsome
fortune for a scoundrel who is not fit for anything else.

Such abuse of the method might naturally be
expected, but the worst feature of it all is that
it is often used as a machine by the government
in relentlessly crushing out the spirit of nationalism. If a Korean is suspected of keeping alive
the spirit of his forefathers,—not rebellion, for
that would be a hopeless thing at present,—the
government instructs its spies to bring certain
charges against him. Upon the witness of the
spies, he will be imprisoned, his property will be
confiscated, and he will be punished in such a
way as to be disabled for life; or he may even be

executed on the charge of treason." Like the mediæval " Ironwoman " that crushed its victim without bloodshed, this spy system of the Japanese administration in Korea removes from the country the ablest and best educated Koreans without technically violating the regulations of the colonial policy of the Japanese Empire.

The sad feature of the Korean case is that, although the Korean suffers the same hard fate as did the Poles and the Armenians before the European War, his story is unknown to the outside world. The only time when he had a partial hearing before the world's court of public opinion was during the late wholesale arrest and trial of the Korean Christian leaders on the charge of conspiracy against the life of Governor-General Terauchi. This time the news leaked out because it involved several prominent foreign missionaries."

[12] For Japanese prison tortures in Korea, see the Continent, June 13, 27, 1912; Sengman Rhee, "The Christian Persecution in Korea" (Korean, published in Honolulu, T. H.).

[13] For full account, see the Report sent to the Continuation Committee by the missionaries in Korea. Also, consult Arthur Judson Brown, "The Korean Conspiracy Case" (1912); Sengman Rhee, "The Christian Persecution in Korea" (Korean); "A Korean View of Japan's Policy in Korea," Missionary Review of the World, 36: 450-453, June, 1913.

II

THE GOVERNMENT CENSORSHIP

1. Press Censorship

IT is only half a century since Japan abolished feudalism, but the basis of it—loyalty—still remains. This furnishes a fertile ground for the growth and fruition of the political philosophies of Machiavelli and Hegel—the suppression of the individual for the sake of the state. The individual Japanese is not a free citizen, but a tool of the state. He has no conscience of his own except national conscience; he has no liberty except his share in national liberty. The Japanese scholar or publicist is only a mouthpiece of his government. The individuals are for the state, but the state is not for the individuals, as it is in America and Western Europe.[1] This doctrine of individuals ·existing for the sake of the state brings about that unity of purpose and simplicity in ends which are the direct correlatives of national

[1] See W. E. Griffis, " The Mikado—Institution and Person" (1915).

efficiency. Japan is an ambitious climber and an
efficient worker.

With this state-supremacy doctrine in view,
we can understand—incredible though it may
seem to the Western mind—that in Japan the
government outlines its policies, and then forms
the public opinion to support them.[2] Practically
all the publications in the country are more or
less under the control, direct or indirect, of the
government. The native press receives orders
from the government as to the kinds of news
that it should print or suppress. Rigid censorship is in force all the time—not only when
Japan is at war but when Japan is at peace.
" They suppress not only governmental matters
but anything that, in the light of their opinion
of their standing outside, will tend to lower that
estimate which they think the rest of the world
has of them."[3] The following is a typical order
issued by the government with reference to
something the government does not want
printed. In this case it happens to be one concerning the navy, but its precision and thor-
oughness are typical of all orders concerning
even the least important matters.

" By an official order of the Navy Department
the following additions have been made to the
clauses of the press censorship: Matters con-

[2] *New Republic,* November 18, 1916, p. 66.
[3] *Saturday, Evening Post,* May 22, 1915, p. 53.

cerning the naval movements of the ally in war, which have some reference to the naval strategies of the Empire; plans of war; organizations of fleets and ships, their duties, present condition and movements; employing of transports, their crews, their present condition and their movements; whereabouts of fleets and transport ships, and their departure and arrival; as to goods ordered for service; the naval preparations and defenses in naval stations and along the coast; present condition of the various companies engaged in manufacturing war materials for the navy by order of the naval arsenal and the Navy Department; the positions and names of the bases or gathering places; the same regulations as to aeroplanes. Beside the foregoing, anything that has not been made public by the government and has direct or indirect reference to naval secrets."[4]

Such a thing as a constitutional guarantee of a free press is an unheard-of liberty in Japan. After the Japanese occupation of Korea, all the Korean dailies and magazines were suppressed under one pretext after another, and were gradually abolished.[5] In their places the government established one subsidized daily published

[4] Order issued in September, 1914, quoted by Samuel G. Blythe, *Saturday Evening Post*, May 22, 1915.
[5] See Park, " The Tragic History of Korea " (Chinese edition, Shanghai), Sec. 3, chap. 36.

in Korean, *Mai Ill Shin Po,* which zealously scatters far and wide among the natives the doctrine of obedience and loyalty. The Japanese even propose to establish a Korean daily in Hawaii to fight the *Korean National Herald* in Honolulu.[*]

In forming public opinion both at home and abroad to support its policies, the Japanese Government utilizes not only the native press, but also the foreign publications in Japan. Many prominent English journals published in Japan are owned by Japanese.[†] Most of the others are edited by those pro-Japanese foreigners who have some interest in Japan, financial or otherwise. Take, for example, the *Japan Daily Mail,* perhaps the most powerful English daily in the Far East. Its founder and former editor was Captain Frank Brinkley, a well-known Irishman, formerly in the Japanese Government service, and later foreign adviser to the largest Japanese shipping company, the Nippon Yusen Kaisha. Concerning Captain Brinkley's relation with the Japanese, a prominent English journalist writes as follows:

" Captain Brinkley's great knowledge of Japanese life and language is admitted and admired by all. His independence of judgment is, however, weakened by his close official connection

[*] *Korean National Herald,* editorial, November 29, 1916.
[†] *Japan Magazine, Herald of Asia,* etc.

with the Japanese Government and by his personal interest in Japanese industry. His journal is regarded generally as a government mouthpiece, and he has succeeded in making himself a more vigorous advocate of the Japanese claims than even the Japanese themselves. It can safely be forecasted that whenever a dispute arises between Japanese and British interests Captain Brinkley and his journal will play the part, through thick and thin, of defenders of the Japanese." [8]

The above might be said of nearly all the foreign editors in Japan. When Japan began the wholesale arrest of the Korean Christian leaders and educators in 1911–1912, on the charge of a conspiracy, the Associated Press agent refused to send out the reports of the trial, except in so far as favourable to the Japanese. James Gordon Bennett, the owner of the *New York Herald*, ordered J. K. Ohl, the *Herald's* experienced and trustworthy correspondent at Peking, to proceed to Seoul and report the details of the "Conspiracy Trial." Mr. Ohl's reports demonstrated that the Associated Press was less than fair to the Koreans and a little more than fair to the Japanese. Immediately great pressure was brought to bear by the Associated Press on the *New York Herald*, and the latter was forced to say editorially that it was convinced that "the

[8] F. A. McKenzie, "The Tragedy of Korea," p. 216.

Associated Press reports were truthful and adequate," which was a virtual apology on the part of the *New York Herald* for sending its own able correspondent to report the trial instead of printing the sifted news doled out by the pro-Japanese agent of the Associated Press. A New York weekly, commenting on this, says editorially:

" The external appearance of the case strongly indicates that the threat bringing *The Herald* thus to its knees was some intimation that its own news franchise in the Associated Press was in jeopardy of being revoked. . . . If the Associated Press management can make such a powerful metropolitan daily as *The Herald* ' eat crow ' . . . what can it not do by way of dictation and repression with others of its constituent papers, which, to say the least, cannot be more capable of resisting it than *The New York Herald* is? " [9]

After the reports of the " Conspiracy Trial " were brought out to the West largely through missionary channels, the Associated Press agent, J. Russell Kennedy, who garbled the reports of the case, was no longer able to hold his position as an unbiased press agent. He resigned his position from the Associated Press, and the Japanese Government promptly awarded his loyal service to Japan by making him the head of the

[9] *The Continent,* January 9, 1913.

Koksai (Japanese National News Agency) at Tokyo.

It might be said that pro-Japanese policy is adopted as a matter of expediency on the part of some of the journals in Japan. The Japanese Government encourages and gives all kinds of aid, direct and indirect, to those newspapers that follow its policy, but insidiously suppresses foreign publications that do not serve its purpose. The pressure is so strong that no single journal can successfully resist it. The case of the late E. T. Bethell and the *Korea Daily News* may be cited as an example of the usual fate of an independent foreign newspaper in the Japanese Empire.

In the summer of 1904, Mr. Bethell, a young English journalist, settled in Seoul as temporary correspondent of a London daily paper, and started a modest bilingual journal, the *Korea Daily News*, printed partly in English and partly in Korean. He did not hesitate to record the facts as he saw them, regardless of their palatable nature to the Japanese. This brought him into direct conflict with the Japanese authorities. For a time it was doubtful whether he could withstand the pressure. "The Japanese were making his life as uncomfortable as they possibly could, and were doing everything to obstruct his work. His mails were constantly tampered with; his servants were threatened or arrested on various excuses, and his household was subjected to the closest espionage. He displayed surprising tenacity, and held on month after month without showing any sign of yielding." [10]   He was approached with threat, cajolery, bribe and everything, in fact, the Japanese could think of to win him over to their side. But the English journalist stood his ground like a stone wall.

Failing to conciliate the editor, the Japanese sought to cut the ground from under his feet by starting an opposition paper printed in English. An able Japanese journalist, Mr. Zumoto, became the editor.   With the financial backing of the Japanese Government, this new journal, the *Seoul Press*, started out in fine shape, and was distributed almost for nothing.   But the *Korea Daily News* held more than its own.   Finally diplomacy was brought into play, and this young English journalist was ordered to leave the country and the *Korea Daily News* was suppressed by the order of the British Foreign Office." [11]

2.   Censorship of Postal and Telegraphic Communications

Prior to the opening of the World War there were three general news telegraph services op-

[10] McKenzie, " The Tragedy of Korea," p. 213.
[11] For full discussion, see McKenzie, " The Tragedy of Korea," chap. XIX.

erating to and from the Far East: Reuter (British), Ostasiatische Lloyd and its connections (German), and the Koksai (Japanese National News Agency). Of these the Reuter system was the most powerful and, perhaps, the least biased, although in times past, this agency has been accused on many occasions of fulfilling the function of keeping a certain point of view to the fore; and of obscuring, minimizing, or suppressing altogether the opposite or contrary points of view, according to the wishes of the British Government. The British Government grants special low telegraphic toll to this service, and being a British concern, it is altogether probable that the news gathered and distributed by this agency is, consciously or unconsciously, somewhat coloured in favour of the British, both as a matter of business expediency and of patriotism. But the Koksai is aided by the Japanese Government to such an extent that no other news-gathering agency can compete with it in Japan and in her territories. On February 1, 1914, an agreement to coöperate was made between the Koksai and Reuter, with the approval of the foreign offices of both the British and Japanese Governments. It was agreed that Reuter service from Japan should be entirely supplied by the Koksai. This gives the semi-official news-telegraphic service of Japan a double advantage: the Koksai can send out news items direct to other countries, or it can have the Reuter perform the service, in case of any advantage to the Japanese. Being the sole news-gathering agency in the country, the Koksai can handle the news as it sees fit—minimize or magnify, suppress or create. When there is an item of news that cannot be sent out without betraying the hand of the government behind it, then the Koksai, instead of sending it directly to foreign countries, hands the item over to the Reuter service in the Far East which "sprinkles it through the press, English and vernacular, east of Suez, and carries it to London, where it will be picked up by American correspondents and services and passed along," as news coming from the *English* news-gathering agency.[12]

No dispatch can go in or out of the Japanese Empire unless it has the sanction of the government. Any incoming news that does not agree with the policy of the government is suppressed. A month before the opening of hostilities between Japan and Russia the Japanese cut off communication between Port Arthur and the Russian Legation at Seoul, so that M. Pavloff, then Russian minister to Korea, was forced to use a special war-ship to communicate with Port Arthur. When Count Lamsdorf sent his tele-

[12] From an editorial in *China Press* (Shanghai), October 13, 1914.

gram to Baron Rosen, the Russian minister to Japan, in February, 1904, it was delayed three days before delivery.[13]

The control of the outgoing dispatches is even more complete than that of the incoming. When the Korean Queen was murdered by the Japanese Government assassins in 1895, Colonel Cockerill, the famous correspondent of the *New York Herald*, was in Seoul. At once he cabled the news to his paper, but his message was stopped and the money returned to him.[14] At the time of the destruction of Korean independence, it was impossible for the Korean Government to lodge a formal protest with the powers, because of the complete control of communication by the Japanese.

The official supervision of the telegraphic-news service gives the Japanese Government an ample opportunity to create as well as to suppress news, either for home or foreign consumption. The part played by President Roosevelt at the Portsmouth Conference between Russia and Japan was really a service to Japan, as the Eastern Empire, although assuming the attitude of a victor, was at the end of her financial strain and was anxious for peace. The results of the conference were disappointing to the people who had been led by their press and govern-

[13] The Russian Circular Note, issued March 12, 1904.
[14] McKenzie, "The Tragedy of Korea," p. 67.

ment to entertain high hopes and to make free sacrifices for the war. Instead of letting the people know the truth, the government created an impression among them through its publicity channels that the meddling of the United States was robbing Japan of substantial fruits of victory, and that the people should not hesitate to make further sacrifices for the creating and maintaining of a bigger army and navy which alone could vindicate Japan's rights in the future —especially against the United States. "If publicity is wanted in the Far East, some publication in China frequently is used. For instance, soon after Japan declared war against Germany a report was published in the *Fengtien Daily News* on August 9, 1914, that an American fleet had been dispatched to the Far East to protect China against Japan. Japan's vernacular organs in China spread this report, and caused some excitement among the Chinese. The report was telegraphed to Tokyo, and for a while it served as a topic for bitter editorial criticism of the United States. When denial was made by the United States, the Japanese press had to drop the matter; and it then side-stepped responsibility by charging the origin of the report to Germany. The facts seem to be that the report originated in Japan, with the purpose of using it for all it was worth to stir up popular feeling there against America, then accuse Germany of

inciting it; thus making it serve the various purposes of further stimulating Japanese resentment
against America, rousing American resentment
against Germany, and warning Chinese against
alleged German and American intrigues." [15]

The government interception of private mail
is not less thorough than the control of dispatches.   It is not a war measure or military
necessity, but a part of the established system
of national administration.   A short account
given by Samuel G. Blythe, concerning the in-
discriminate opening of private mail, is interesting and to the point.   It follows:

" An official in the Department of Communication, whom I happen to know, told me with
great pride, when I was in Japan, that they had
just secured from Russia a machine which made
the work of opening and reading letters much
easier.   The former method was to steam the
letters open, read them, copy them if desired,
and seal them again.   This Russian machine, as
I understand it, has a blade of great thinness
and keenness.   It slits the envelope in such a
manner that the cut is barely perceptible along
the edge of the envelope.   Then the writing is
taken out, read, copied and replaced or destroyed; and the edges are rubbed and stuck together by the machine in such a way that the
fact that they have been cut is not discernible.

[15] Millard, " Our Eastern Question," pp. 213–214.

I asked this man why they went to such great trouble:

" ' Everybody who knows anything about the inside workings of the Japanese Government knows that all letters they want to read are opened and read anyhow. Why take such elaborate precautions to hide that fact? ' I said.

" ' My dear sir,' he replied, ' it is contrary to the practice of our government to disclose these things.'

" Japan always has opened letters. . . . No one can object if a government opens letters that may contain information of use to an enemy; but why should letters be opened indiscriminately? " [16]

It goes without saying that such a system is highly annoying to foreigners in Japan and Korea. Even missionaries, the most subservient and non-complaining of all Westerners in the Far East, have complained of the Japanese interception of their mail.[17]

But the heaviest blow of the system falls on the Koreans. In Korea, under the Japanese military administration, the system is not covered up, but openly practiced. Both the writer and receiver of letters objectionable to the government are punished. I know of more than

[16] *Saturday Evening Post*, May 22, 1915.
[17] See W. T. Ellis, " Christianity's Fiery Trial in Korea," *The Continent*, June 27, 1912, pp. 896–899.

one case in which confiscation of property took place on the charge of this " treasonable crime."

This overt punishment for writing objectionable letters may be said to be another point of Japanese cleverness in the abolition of the Korean nationality. For it creates an atmosphere of fear, which suppresses almost unconsciously everything that pertains to Korean independence or nationality, or anything that intimates criticism of the Japanese administration in the peninsula. No Korean in America or in any other foreign country dare write anything in the least questionable in his letters to his friends at home, not because of himself but for the sake of those receiving them.[18]

[18] See *Missionary Review of the World,* June, 1913, vol. 36: pp. 450–453.

III

PUBLICITY PROPAGANDA

1. OFFICIAL PUBLICATIONS

THERE is a remarkable similarity between the German publicity propaganda, as it was disclosed at the beginning of the European War, and the Japanese publicity propaganda; only the Japanese method is far subtler than the German. *Fatherland,* formerly published in New York, once characterized Dr. Eliot, the president emeritus of Harvard, as " Foxy Eliot," for the stand he took with regard to the belligerents. A Japanese organ would never have done this, for the Japanese have enough knowledge of American psychology to know that such an attack on one of the most venerable educators in the country would produce an effect contrary to that intended. This instance is cited to illustrate the difference between the Japanese and the German methods.

The government publishes or authorizes private concerns to publish year books, annual

144

reports, statistical abstracts, in foreign languages, not to inform, but to misinform the outside world. Many writers in America and Europe have paid unreserved tribute to Japan as the wisest colonial administrator of to-day.[1] They base their information on *Report on Reforms and Progress in Chosen*, an annual published in English by the Japanese administration in Korea. From the standpoint of those who know the actual condition of Korea to-day, this Japanese publication is highly amusing, for it gives the reader an impression that, all the way from Imperial Rome down to the American Commonwealth, there never was a nation so wise, just, and humanitarian to a subject people as the Japanese are to the Koreans. Indeed, the words of Colonel Cockerill have lost nothing of their force since they were penned in 1895, after the Korean Queen was murdered by the Japanese assassins.

" I decline to believe anything in the shape of news sent out by the correspondents of the Japanese newspapers," wrote the famous American correspondent. " A more flagitious and unconscionable lot of liars I have never known. As the Japanese Government exercises a strong censorship over its home press, it might be well for it to try its repressional hand upon the Jap-

[1] See " Korea—A Tribute to Japan," *Review of Reviews,* 52: 232–233, August, 1915.

anese sheet published in Seoul, the *Kanjo-shimpo*, which is labouring zealously, it would seem, to bring about the massacre of foreign representatives in Korea."[2]

The rapid spread of the pacifist movement prior to the opening of the European War was taken advantage of by the Japanese and used effectively to shield their military ambitions and to discourage the increase of armaments in America. Eminent pacifists like David Starr Jordan visited Japan and brought back reports as to the national sentiment of the Japanese people to the effect that the ultimate aim of Japan is peace, not war; that "war talk on either side is foolish and criminal. Japan recognizes the United States as her nearest neighbour among Western nations, her best customer and most steadfast friend. . . . For the future greatness of Japan depends on the return of the old peace with 'velvet-sandalled feet,' which made her the nation she is to-day."[3] But if we look the facts squarely in the face despite the statement of officials and public men of Japan to the contrary, the American Peace Society of Japan, the Japan Peace Society, and many other similar organizations are nothing more than the catspaw of the Japanese national program. The actions and work of these societies have no

[2] Quoted by McKenzie in "The Tragedy of Korea," p. 77.
[3] David Starr Jordan, "War and Waste," pp. 150–151.

effect upon the policy of Japan, nor do they
check the rapid growth of Japan's militarism,
although they have influenced American public
opinion and have retarded, to a certain extent,
naval and military preparations on the part of
the United States. Count Okuma is a powerful
imperialist; he is liberal in internal affairs, but
decidedly Bismarckian in foreign policy. In an
article published in *Shin Nijon* (May, 1915), he
wrote: "Diplomacy, to be really effective and
successful, must be backed up by sufficient national strength. It is only ten or fifteen years
since Japanese diplomacy began to carry weight
with foreign countries, and it began from the
time that Western Powers commenced to recognize Japan's military strength." Yet this
Elder Statesman is the President of the Japan
Peace Society which depicts Japan to the Western public as posing in an attitude of naïve paci-
fism. A paragraph from an editorial comment
on the annual meeting and report of the American Peace Society of Japan by the most independent British daily in Japan is illuminating
and to the point:

"Clearly there is some incongruity in the
American Peace Society of Japan deploring the
increase of armaments in the United States
while absolutely silent on the expansion of the
Japanese army this year by two divisions, and
the impending program for the enlargement of

the Japanese navy. . . . It is curious, indeed,
that even the Japan Peace Society, which num-
bers Japanese as well as foreigners among its
members, and has as its president Count Okuma,
never seems to consider it essential to oppose
the expansion of armaments in Japan or to dep-
recate the chauvinism so often exhibited in Japanese newspapers and public statements. So
far as we have observed, the Japan Peace Society has never passed a single resolution against
the enlargement of the Japanese army or the
increase of the navy, nor has it uttered a word
in depreciation of the hostile action which the
government is often urged to take against
China. It seems to be chiefly concerned in the
attitude of other countries toward Japan, especially of America, the dangers of militarism and
armaments in this country being wholly ignored.
Again, the Japan Society of America, also concerned in the maintenance of good relations between Japan and the United States, some time
ago published a 'Symposium of Papers by Political Leaders and Representative Citizens of
Japan on the Relations Between Japan and the
United States.' Some of the declarations in
that are of the most chauvinistic nature. Mr.
Takekoshi, a journalist and M. P., says that
'Korea exists now for Japan, from the view-
point of imperial policy,' and demands the development of Manchuria also. Another prominent

journalist in an article entitled, 'Centripetal
Mikadoism,' shows himself a flamboyant imperialist. . . . A peace society in Japan which con-
centrates all its attention on menaces to peace
abroad while ignoring those at its own doors
may be adopting a very prudent policy, but it is
not contributing much to the cause of international good will."[4]

It is interesting in this connection to note how
the Japanese handle figures. According to the
figures received by the Western statisticians,
the Korean population in 1912, two years after
the annexation, was 13,461,299. By December
31, 1915, this figure had jumped to 17,405,645,
exclusive of Japanese and Chinese.[5] This ge-
netic increase of 3,944,346 people in three years
speaks eloquently for the beneficence of Japanese rule in Korea. Here, the Japanese, past
masters as they are in the art of deception, have
overreached themselves. They explain that the
more hygienic living and better economic well-
being under the Japanese rule are the causes of
the suddenly high birth-rate and the correspondingly sudden lowering of the death-rate. Even
if that were granted, an annual increase of ap-
proximately 9.8 per cent. is inconceivable with
any people. In Japan itself, during the past five

[4] *Japan Chronicle,* December 21, 1915.
[5] Figures taken from the *Statesman's Year Book,* 1913,
1916.

years the annual increase of population did not exceed 1.3 per cent. In Germany, between 1905 and 1910, where the race is most prolific and the economic conditions for the growth of population have been nearly ideal, the annual increase was only 1.36 per cent.[6] Such manipulation of figures with regard to the Korean population brought a vigorous protest from Dr. Sengman Rhee, the editor of the *Korean Pacific Magazine*.

" Genetically, the Korean people have been a static race for several hundred years," wrote Dr. Rhee. " Since the Japanese occupation of the country they were put under severe economic strain. They were driven out of former occupations to make room for the incoming Japanese. Hundreds of native firms went bankrupt, because they were unable to meet the Japanese competitors backed by the administration. More than three hundred thousand Koreans emigrated to China since Korea lost her identity as a nation. It is a sociological law that in hard times people postpone marriage and the birth-rate drops. And the Korean people are no exception to this rule. There is all the reason to believe that the Korean population during the last five years would have decreased rather than increased. Although I have no definite proof to make a positive statement, yet it is very

[6] *Statesman's Year Book,* 1916.

probable that the Japanese, with their characteristic foresight in deception, gave out an un-
der-estimate in 1912 with the view of increasing
it in a few years. The traditional population of
Korea was twenty million, and it could not have
been any less than seventeen million at the time
of annexation." [1]

" In the East, in perhaps a greater degree
than elsewhere," writes Mr. Millard, the editor
of the *China Press* and the author of many important books on the Far Eastern problems,
" statistics often are prepared to sustain an hy-
pothesis. This is especially true, at the present
time, of some statistics which relate to the economic and fiscal situation of Japan." [8]

2.   GOVERNMENT AGENCIES IN FOREIGN LANDS

What is left undone, in the way of publicity,
by the press and official publications is accomplished by the semi-official agencies in the West.
From the Japanese bureau of information in
New York, or from the one in San Francisco,
an American can get information on any matter
concerning Japan; but it is the strict policy of
the bureau to give out only what the Japanese
Government wishes to have believed in the
West.[9]

[1] *Korean Pacific Magazine,* editorial, October, 1916.
[8] " The Far Eastern Question," Introduction.
[9] The official title of the New York Bureau is " East and
West News Bureau." It is maintained for promoting a

The Japan Society of New York is another medium of dissemination of everything Japanese. It was organized in May, 1907. At present it boasts an active membership of over a thousand people including such eminent men as Seth Low, Hamilton Holt, William Elliot Griffis, Elbert H. Gary, and Jokichi Takamine. American libraries are flooded with the bulletins and pamphlets of the Japan Society, all distributed gratuitously.

In addition to these sources of propaganda, there are paid lecturers and writers who take every opportunity to placate the Western opinion and present Japan in the most favourable light. Although scholars like Inazo Nitobe have travelled in the United States as professorial lecturers, in reality they have told their college audiences in America what the Japanese Government or newspaper could not publish without betraying its motive.[10] The Japanese scholar is, in reality, a co-worker with and a mouthpiece of his government. In 1916, when Japan deliberately attempted to veto the contract to repair the Grand Canal in Shantung,

better understanding between America and Japan. Dr. T. Iyenaga, a professorial lecturer at Columbia University, is the Director of the Bureau. The one in San Francisco is known as the "Pacific Press Bureau," headed by K. K. Kawakami.

[10] A collection of lectures by Dr. Nitobe, "The Japanese Nation—Its Land, Its People and Its Life," distributed gratuitously by the Japan Society, New York.

granted by the Chinese Government to an American corporation, and failed, the well-known Director of the East and West News Bureau, Dr. T. Iyenaga, lost no time in offering an apologetic excuse for his government:

" If it is true that Japan made any protest to the railway scheme and the reconstruction in China of the Grand Canal to be undertaken by American capital, I am inclined to think that it is simply to put on record the priority of Japan's rights in an undertaking of that kind within the Province of Shantung. . . . So far as Japan is concerned, I am sure she welcomes the development of China's resources by whomsoever it is undertaken, for such development will certainly tend to enhance the purchasing power of the Chinese, which in turn will react favourably on the Japanese trade in the Chinese market." [11]

The war-ridden attention of America was somewhat diverted in the fall of 1916 by a new set of demands made on China by Japan, known as the " Chengchiatun demands," which the *Peking Gazette* characterized as "A Foot-note to the Twenty-one Demands." [12] It was believed that the trouble was concocted by the Japanese military authorities in China in order to furnish a cause for such demands by the Tokyo Govern-

[11] *Japan Society Bulletin*, No. 35, p. 67, November 30, 1916.
[12] *Peking Gazette*, September 9, 1916.

ment. After the fall of the Okuma Ministry,
Premier Terauchi and his associates withdrew
the demands as a matter of expediency in dealing with the Chinese. At present, they thought,
a lenient policy toward China would be more
beneficial to Japan than military bullying. This
furnished a golden opportunity to bring Japan
out once again into the limelight of American
public opinion—to show the West the splendid
spirit of sacrifice and the magnanimity of Japan.
Japan, as a nation, never hesitates to admit its
mistakes, if there be any, and rectify its wrongs,
—so the Japanese publicists in this country
would tell us. The following is a paragraph
from the pen of K. K. Kawakami, the best
known Japanese author and editor in America,
on the withdrawal of the " Chengchiatun demands."

" However disagreeable such admission may
be to Japan, we must frankly confess that many
of the recent troubles, resulting from the contact of Japanese and Chinese upon Chinese soil,
have been caused by *China ronin* (professional
Japanese agitators in China) as well as by unau-
thorized actions of army men over whom the
civilian premier had only inadequate power." [13]

Had the cause and nature of the demands not
been known in America and had the Tokyo
Government sustained the demands, Mr. Kawa-

[13] *Review of Reviews,* February, 1917, p. 179.

kami or any other Japanese writer would prob-
ably never have said the above. But as it was,
the occasion was taken advantage of to reveal
Japan in an attitude of innocent repentance and
sacrifice, and also to create an impression that
the Japanese spokesmen in America are frank
and outspoken in criticizing their own government. It is a curious fact that no Japanese publicist raised a single point of criticism of his government for making the "Twenty-one De-
mands" upon China in 1915,—the demands
which were far more serious than the "Chengchiatun demands" in impairing the political independence and territorial integrity of China.
On the contrary, writers like Mr. Kawakami
misrepresented the facts of the "Twenty-one
Demands," and attempted to convince the
American public that Japan was making the demands with an "unselfish motive to aid China."[14]

Besides the Japanese, there are a few Westerners in the service of the Japanese Government to help in their publicity propaganda.
"Paid agents lectured English audiences upon
the beauties and glories of Nippon."[15] Honorary Consuls are appointed not so much to make

[14] See K. K. Kawakami, "What Can Japan Do For
China?" *Independent*, 82: 280–281, May 17, 1915. A complete record of Japan's Twenty-one Demands made upon
China in 1915, and the various steps taken in connection
with them are given in Millard, "Our Eastern Question,"
chapters on "Japan's Aggressions in China."
[15] McKenzie, "The Tragedy of Korea," p. 105.

trade reports or look after Japanese commercial interests, but mainly to coöperate with the larger national system and play the local part in the publicity game.[16] Thus nothing is left undone; what is overlooked by the national worker is taken up by his local associates. " When it comes to publicity," said an American journalist, " the Japanese catch us in every direction."

3. Manipulation of Foreign Visitors in Japan

The remarkable success of the Japanese propaganda in controlling the public opinion of America has been due largely to the coöperation of public men on this side of the ocean. All the praise we hear of Nippon from the lecture platforms and in periodical literature would have come to naught if it were not endorsed by public men in this country who visit Japan and bring back favourable reports. The Japanese have shown consummate skill in manipulating the distinguished foreigners who visit Japan.

The Japan Society in America maintains a Travel Bureau, issues letters of introduction and publishes descriptive travel pamphlets which supplement the official traveller's guide published by the Japanese Government. The minute a globe-trotter lands in Japan he has little

[16] There are Japanese Honorary Consuls in New Orleans, St. Louis, Denver, Mobile. Galveston, Philadelphia, and Boston. They are all Americans.

chance to see or find out anything for himself, especially if he is a distinguished personage. He is met at the pier by a polished guide conversant with Western manners and language; he is directed to a hotel; is shown about with great kindness and courtesy. He is impressed by the politeness and hospitality of the people and is charmed by the beautiful scenes and unique festivals of the land. The country seems to him a land of poets, artists and lovers, where the lotus blooms and life is a happy dream of ease and devotion to the service of art. His sense of admiration and wonder increases when he is shown the accomplishments of modern Japan— the army, navy, commerce, industry. Here is a land where the military virtues are fostered without losing sight of the beautiful; where there is industry without sordid materialism; wealth without the idle rich. The Japanese are the most well balanced of all races, the visitors write home. " They have become practical, but they still love the cherry tree and write poems to it; they are developing great business activities, but they continue to paint with almost unrivalled delicacy and precision; they support a strong army and navy, but both are kept in high efficiency for defensive purposes." [11]

" It was delightful," said an American gentle-

[11] See articles by Hamilton W. Mabie, "Japan To-day and To-morrow," in the *Outlook*, vols. 103, 104, 1913.

man after his visit to Japan. "I never enjoyed myself so much. Every time I wanted to go anywhere there was an automobile at my disposal and a Japanese official to show me about and explain things to me. I was constantly attended and made comfortable; and I was given unexampled opportunities for seeing Japan, and guided to all the points of interest, and had the real Japanese spirit explained to me by cultivated Japanese officials and scholars. My view of Japan has entirely changed. I now realize how great is the work they are doing, how patriotic they are, how wonderful as a people!"

"Their methods when a distinguished American gets to Japan are interesting and efficacious," wrote Samuel G. Blythe, after his return from Japan in 1915. "Their hospitality is unbounded; their courtesy is unexampled; their attentions are flattering; their polite recognition and deference are alluring to the susceptible. The Japanese capture a distinguished American without half trying. They have become experts at the game." [18]

The distinguished foreigner is kept constantly on the move; is dined, wined, and entertained; is invited to give addresses; is taken here and there; is made much of; in certain cases, deemed most important by the Japanese, he is presented to the Emperor or given a decoration. It is

[18] *Saturday Evening Post*, May 22, 1915.

said that when Vice-President Fairbanks was in Korea, the Japanese authorities tried their utmost to keep him busy with the official functions of the government so as to prevent him from having private conversations with resident Americans.[19] In 1909, when Lord Kitchener went through Korea, an English resident, who was an old friend of Kitchener, tried to invite the distinguished visitor to his home for dinner, but the Japanese officials refused the privilege on the ground that the details of his visit and entertainment had already been arranged.

When Judge Elbert H. Gary went to Japan in 1916, he was met on board the ship by the Japanese reception committee. His special train was to arrive at Tokyo at twilight, so that the procession could pass through a mammoth electric arch with the sign, " Welcome, Judge and Mrs. Gary." The Chairman of the United States Corporation was interviewed by distinguished Japanese statesmen and financiers; was invited to give addresses; was entertained at luncheons, banquets, and receptions given in his honour; and was shown about the country with characteristic Japanese deference and hospitality. An American journalist who knows the Japanese method of capturing distinguished foreigners spoke of the Judge at that time as being " one of the biggest fishes that got caught

[19] See *The Continent*, June 27, 1912, p. 897.

in the net of the Japanese publicity propaganda for some time." In describing Japanese hospitality after his return to America, the steel magnate said, " I have never before seen it excelled nor even equalled. An American gentleman, if he is known and considered worthy and representative, will receive invitations by Marconi for luncheons or dinners or other functions from those who are in office or have been in some way designated to speak for the sentiment of the people; he will be met on the ship before it is docked by a committee or delegation from the city he is approaching; and from the time he lands upon Japanese territory until he departs he will receive the kindest and most liberal hospitality that can be offered, and always with a grace and charm and simplicity that cannot be surpassed. . . . I have no doubt that the leading and controlling men in Japan earnestly desire to maintain cordial, close and continuous relations with the people of the United States. It seems to me, if we ever have serious trouble with Japan it will be as much the fault of the United States as it is the fault of Japan; and perhaps more." [20] The Japan Society of America gathered all the addresses delivered by Judge Gary in Japan, bound them in an attractive pamphlet, *Japan as Viewed by*

[20] From address delivered at the Bankers' Club, New York, November 9, 1916 (pamphlet mentioned).

Judge Elbert H. Gary, and scattered it gratis to all
the leading libraries in the country as the sane
and unbiased view of a distinguished American
business man. When the United States declared its policy of embargo on steel in 1917,
Baron Shibusawa, the leading Japanese finan-
cier and semi-official spokesman of his government, sent the appeal of the Japanese industrial
concerns direct to Judge Gary to see to it that
Japan might be exempted from the embargo.[21]
Indeed, the American steel magnate wielded a
powerful influence in bringing about the arrangement by which Japan could get steel from
the United States, as usual, in return for furnishing shipping in the Pacific so that the American vessels there could be transferred to the
Atlantic for war purposes.

The average globe-trotter in Japan sees Japan
through the eyes of the Japanese. He sees
nothing except what the Japanese want him to
see, and hears nothing except what the Japanese want him to hear. " No condition can
arise in Japan whereby a foreigner can learn
from a Japanese of anything to the detriment
of the country. The statesmen will not tell you
anything. The coolies will not tell you anything. They are units of concealment. They
put the good face on everything. . . . If

[21] Telegram given to the press by Judge Gary, New York,
October 8, 1917.

you ask a Japanese to read you from a Japanese newspaper, he will carefully skip anything he may find in that paper that, as it seems to him, would be detrimental to the fair name and fame of Japan if communicated to a foreigner. If a Japanese—any Japanese—hears anything he deems of importance or of use to his country, he sees to it that that information gets to the proper person. He seeks to show you the bright spots." [22] Indeed, the late Richard Harding Davis characterized the Japanese method of showing Japan to the Westerner as like telling a young woman that she might go out to swim but she mustn't go near the water." [23]

This unprecedented manipulation of foreign visitors, the peculiar trait of the Japanese, has far-reaching consequences in forming public opinion in the West with regard to Oriental politics. Few, if any, escape the Japanese net of hospitality and bring back true reports. The majority of foreigners leave Japan in a happy haze of pleasant impressions and ever afterward sing the joys and beauties and wonders of the country. They form a bulwark of Japanese defense in the public sentiment in the West; persistently refuse to believe anything that is disparaging to their once kind and generous host; and in some cases, they become more vigorous

[22] Samuel G. Blythe, *Saturday Evening Post*, May 1, 1915.
[23] See " The Russo-Japanese War," chap. VII, " The Chroniclers of War."

advocates of the rights of *Dai Nippon* than the
Japanese themselves. Especially is this notice-
able on the part of publicists, such as George
Kennan, the well-known American journalist,
who received an unlimited hospitality during his
stay in Japan, and Dr. George Trumbull Ladd,
who was made an honorary member of the Imperial Educational Society of Japan and was
twice decorated by the late Emperor with the
insignias of the Rising Sun.[24]

The " Twenty-one Demands " made on China
by Japan on January 18, 1915, is one of the most
notorious pieces of international robbery in
modern times. Had China conceded to the
terms as they were first presented by Mr. Hioki,
the Japanese minister at Peking, the ancient
Empire would be a vassal state to-day. The demands were first presented by the Japanese
Government to the Chinese coupled with a
strong admonition to China that both haste and
secrecy were required in this consideration.
Continuous pressure was brought on China to
force her to concede the demands *en bloc* without
discussion, and the Chinese officials were warned
not to inform other powers of the demands and
negotiations, even confidentially. The Japanese
Government officially denied, as being utterly
false, all press reports in China about the de-

[24] Mr. Kennan's articles on Japan in the *Outlook,* and Dr.
Ladd's "In Korea With Marquis Ito," and "Benevolent
Assimilation," are decidedly pro-Japanese.

mands. Newspapers in Japan were warned by
the government not to publish or discuss news
of the demands, and Japan's diplomatic representatives abroad were instructed to deny and
discredit any such news. The Japanese minister at Peking stated in response to inquiries
of other foreign ministers that no demands had
been made. When copies of the original demands, procured from the Chinese Government,
were received by foreign governments, Japan
still denied the twenty-one demands, and gave
out a list of eleven articles, omitting the most
objectionable matters, as " friendly " demands
made by Japan upon China " in accordance with
the principle of the maintenance of the territorial integrity of China."

As the facts of the case began to leak out,
those who knew something about the political
situation in the East were nonplussed at the
callous selfishness of Japan. " Her statesmen
have set truth and common decency at defiance
in a way unparalleled in the most torturous
diplomacy of the worst courts of the vilest
period of history," [25] as the *National Review*
(Shanghai) expressed it. Others refused to
believe the reports as being utterly incredible.
At this time Dr. Shailer Mathews returned from
Japan and made a report that " much of the
news emanating from Peking is obviously

[25] Quoted in *Review of Reviews*, 52: 230, August, 1915.

coloured by anti-Japanese feeling, and it is difficult to accept any of the reports on their face value; and this colouring of reports in the apparent interest of making trouble between the United States and Japan is a menace." An influential New York weekly shrewdly compared the Japanese policy in China with the Monroe Doctrine of the United States and said, " The Monroe Doctrine . . . was adopted as a means of self-protection, and has never been made an excuse for aggrandizement or interference in the governmental policies of American Republics. The policy of Japan may be likened to that of Monroe Doctrine so far as it seeks to protect itself through checking European aggressions." [26]

China waited and stood the pressure as long as she was able, and finally conceded the demands slightly modified, giving Japan the paramount sphere of influence in China. " She could not help herself. She had to give way. But to say that her giving way and Japan's paltry modifications of her demands have brought about a peaceful solution is to talk the sheerest drivel," said an English journal published in the Far East." [27]

When the terms of settlement were fully

[26] *Outlook,* 110: 4, May 5, 1915.
[27] Editorial in *National Review* (Shanghai), quoted in *Review of Reviews,* 52: 231, August, 1915.

known to the West, even the most conservative English writers who were in no position to criticize the British ally in the time of war, expressed their views in unmistakable terms. "Japan has violated, and is now violating, the terms of the Portsmouth Treaty and the Anglo-Japanese Alliance," said J. O. P. Bland. "She is taking possession of China's outlying dependencies and endeavouring to establish the beginnings of overlordship in China proper, simply because, for the moment, there is nothing to prevent her from so doing." [28] Yet the prominent New York weekly commented on the settlement of disputes between China and Japan as follows:

"Americans interested in the welfare of China and Japan will rejoice that, at a time when international differences have brought about half the world into war, these two Oriental countries have adjusted their difficulties on a basis of mutual compromise." [29]

These things are not said to cast any reflection on the New York weekly or on any other pro-Japanese journal in America; they are cited to illustrate the tremendous influence the Japanese exercise over publications in this country, through the agencies that have been mentioned.

[28] *Nineteenth Century,* 78: 1198–1212. November, 1915.
[29] *Outlook,* 110: 121–123, May 19, 1915.

CONCLUSION

COMPARISON OF RUSSIAN AND JAPANESE DIPLOMACY

THE mainland of Asia has been, during the last fifty years, an international grab-bag. Each European nation has scrambled for its share in the sphere of influence and for commercial advantages. The two nations that have been most active in the struggle in eastern Asia are Russia and Japan. But Russia is no longer a menace to the peace of Asia. The Soviet Government may crumble to-morrow, but it is not likely that the people will restore their absolute monarchy. Although militaristic Russia no longer exists, the civilized world is very familiar with the tortuous intrigue and secret diplomacy of the former Russian Government. Therefore, by comparing the present-day Japanese diplomacy with that of Russia under the old régime, the reader will get a clearer understanding of the tactics that are being employed by the Asiatic Empire in her intercourse with other nations. We may profitably make, then, a brief comparison of the

diplomacies of these two Powers in the course
of their expansion, territorial and commercial,
in eastern Asia.

Russian history from the time of Peter the
Great down to the abdication of Czar Nich-
olas II, March 15, 1917, has been a history of
territorial aggrandizement and political exploitation. The diplomacy of such a nation
would necessarily be stained by indelible records
of deceit and treachery. Perhaps writers like
Kipling are justified in designating Russia, until
the opening of the European War, as a black
sheep in the European family of nations, and as
utterly unworthy of British respect and friendship.

Japanese diplomacy, on the other hand, is
subtle and insidious. Its inconsistencies are so
skillfully covered that an ordinary observer cannot notice them at all. The Japanese being the
cleverest imitators in the world, spare no pains
in putting on an appearance of honesty and
frankness in their dealings with other peoples.
In fact, they *are* honest when honesty would
give them greater advantage than dishonesty.
"In the Japanese philosophy of life," said Col-
gate Baker, who was born and brought up in
Japan, "right and wrong are terms of mere expediency. It is right to be honest when honesty
gives you an advantage. It is not wrong to be
dishonest when you would lose by honesty.

There is no conception of right for the sake of right." [1]

It is obvious that Japanese diplomacy is far superior to the crude and brutal Russian diplomacy, in so far as obtaining the goal of their respective national policies is concerned. Whatever is done by Russia is known and criticized by outsiders; but such is not the case in Japanese affairs. "From what I know of Japan, inside and outside," wrote Thomas F. Millard, "I am convinced that Western knowledge of darkest Russia is as the noonday sun to the moon compared to general Western understanding of internal forces which sway the policy of Nippon." [2]

During the past ten years of Japanese expansion, Japan committed national crimes not less horrible than those perpetrated by Russia in the worst period of her history. The military tyranny in Korea has been interpreted in the Western press as a firm and necessary measure. "After the Japanese occupation of Manchuria," wrote an American correspondent who personally investigated the situation, "began the state of affairs which, had it occurred in the Balkans or in Manchuria under Russian control, would quickly have resounded through the

[1] "Real Japanese Character," *Independent,* 56: 641–644, March 24, 1904.
[2] Millard, "The Far Eastern Question," p. 185.

world." ³ The Japanese during their expedition against the Germans in Kiaochow confiscated practically all the property in the Liao-Tung Peninsula. The Shantung railway was not a German property. It was built by the Chinese Government with money borrowed from Germany. Japan confiscated this railway on the pretext that it belonged to Germany.⁴ Dispatches of such nature seldom reach the West, and whatever fragmentary news is smuggled out by individual witnesses is entirely discredited in the Western press. The majority of American editors refuse to believe anything that is contrary to their former opinion of Japan; they take great pleasure in quoting the stock phrases of the Japanese statesmen, "Japan has no ulterior motive, no desire to secure more territory, no thought of depriving China or any other peoples of anything which they now possess," ⁵ which promises, George Bronson Rea, the editor of the *Far Eastern Review,* properly calls "worthless scraps of paper to be torn to shreds and scattered to the winds." ⁶

³ Millard, "The New Far East," p. 146.
⁴ Information given me by Dr. W. J. Hiltner, of the Harvard Medical College in China, who personally investigated the problem before his return to America on furlough, November, 1916. "Tsinan-Tsingtau Railway" is the official name; see Millard, "Our Eastern Question," 109-110, for full discussion.
⁵ Count Okuma's "Message to the American People," *Independent,* 79: 291, August 31, 1914.
⁶ Quoted in *Review of Reviews,* 52: 231, August, 1915.

The respective predicaments of the unfortunate peoples living under the Russian and the Japanese domination are best compared perhaps by Park In Sick, a Korean historian and editor, who fled his country since the Japanese occupation:[1]

"To be a subject race is contemptible at its best. It is the most intolerable of all slavery, when the dominating nation happens to be one like Russia or Japan in which the sense of national conscience plays no part in colonial administration, and which holds colonies purely for material gains. To live under the Russian control is like meeting a lion in an open field. Other people will hear the roar and will sympathize with you at least; you might find a chance to run away from the beast. But to live in a country dominated by Japan is like being shut up in a small room with hundreds of cobras. You have no chance to escape, and the world will not know of your death."

It is but just to admit that Japan is not without some excuse in her sinister foreign policies. The only standard by which we can judge the right or wrong of nations in their mutual dealings is the criterion of world culture—the public opinion of the civilized peoples. So far in hu-

---

[1] Park is a profound scholar in Chinese classics. Ex-Premier Kang Yu-Wei wrote the preface to his widely read book, "The Tragic History of Korea" (Chinese).

man history public sentiment has sanctioned secret and questionable methods of diplomacy as legitimate. What would be looked upon as unpardonable dishonesty between individuals is often considered as a clever piece of diplomacy between nations. A single standard of morality is still an ideal, rather than a reality. Especially is this true with nations swayed by imperial aspirations and deep-seated militarism. Japan, the infant prodigy of the East, ambitious of her future and jealous of her rights, has chosen the expedient rather than the righteous path to reach her place in the sun. Her poets have sung the glory and grandeur of war; her philosophers have praised the valour and virtue of militarism. Her merchants have practiced "dumping" and misrepresentation of goods as a matter of course; her statesmen have adopted the Bismarckian "iron and blood" policy as the only road to national greatness. Japan is no longer the gallant knight she was deemed to be in the earlier years of her national ascendency, setting out to rescue Asia from the European dragon; she is now the armed bully of the East. The Asiatics had looked upon her as their teacher and leader; now their hope and faith are shattered in finding her a merciless conqueror, reigning, sword in hand, over subject races. The Japanese national policy may go through a process of regeneration, as the world society is better organized on the basis of nationality and individual freedom. Perhaps the Western nations, at present, have no right to demand of Japan the principles of justice and humanity, which they themselves do not practice. But they have a right to demand the full knowledge of her policies. Open diplomacy is—and it ought to be—the cry of the age. "The highest reach of injustice," as the wise Plato pointed out over twenty centuries ago, "is to be deemed just when you are not." The Koreans,—and, indeed, all subject races—may submit to injustice, but they ought to have a right to demand, at least, openness on the part of their conquerors.

"E'en in the light let us die, if die we must!"

PART III

Documents in the Case

A

TREATY BETWEEN THE UNITED STATES AND JAPAN

Signed November 22, 1894;
Proclaimed March 21, 1895

THE President of the United States of America and His Majesty the Emperor of Japan, being equally desirous of maintaining the relations of good understanding which happily exist between them, by extending and increasing the intercourse between their respective States, and being convinced that this object cannot better be accomplished than by revising the Treaties hitherto existing between the two countries, have resolved to complete such a revision, based upon principles of equity and mutual benefit, and, for that purpose, have named as their Plenipotentiaries, that is to say: The President of the United States of America, Walter Q. Gresham, Secretary of State of the United States, and His Majesty the Emperor of Japan, Jushii Shinichiro Kurino, of the Order of the Sacred Treasure, and of the Fourth Class; who, after having communicated to each other their full powers, found to be in good and due form, have agreed upon and concluded the following Articles:

ARTICLE I

The citizens or subjects of each of the two High Contracting Parties shall have full liberty to enter, travel, or reside in any part of the territories of the other Contracting Party, and shall enjoy full and perfect protection for their persons and property.

They shall have free access to the Courts of Justice in pursuit and defense of their rights; they shall be at liberty equally with native citizens or subjects to choose and employ lawyers, advocates and representatives to pursue and defend their rights before such Courts, and in all other matters connected with the administrations of justice they shall enjoy all the rights and privileges enjoyed by native citizens or subjects.

In whatever relates to rights of residence and travel; to the possession of goods and effects of any kind; to the succession to personal estate, by will or otherwise, and the disposal of property of any sort and in any manner whatsoever which they may lawfully acquire, the citizens or subjects of each Contracting Party shall enjoy in the territories of the other the same privileges, liberties, and rights, and shall be subject to no higher imposts or charges in these respects than native citizens or subjects, or citizens or subjects of the most favoured nation. The citizens or subjects of each of the Contracting Parties shall enjoy in the territories of the other entire liberty of conscience, and, subject to the laws, ordinances, and regulations, shall enjoy the right of private or public exercise of their worship, and also the right of burying their respective countrymen, according to their religious customs, in such suitable and convenient places as may be established and maintained for that purpose.

They shall not be compelled, under any pretext whatsoever, to pay any charges or taxes other or higher than those that are, or may be paid by native citizens or subjects, or citizens or subjects of the most favoured nation.

The citizens or subjects of either of the Contracting Parties residing in the territories of the other shall be exempted from all compulsory military service, whether in the army, navy, national guard, or militia; from all contributions imposed in lieu of personal service; and from all forced loans or military exactions or contributions.

Article II

There shall be reciprocal freedom of commerce and navigation between the territories of the two High Contracting Parties.

The citizens or subjects of each of the High Contracting Parties may trade in any part of the territories of the other by wholesale or retail in all kinds of produce, manufactures, and merchandise of lawful commerce, either in person or by agents, singly or in partnership with foreigners or native citizens or subjects; and they may there own or hire and occupy houses, manufactories, warehouses, shops and premises which may be necessary for them, and lease land for residential and commercial purposes, conforming themselves to the laws, police and customs regulations of the country like native citizens or subjects.

They shall have liberty freely to come with their ships and cargoes to all places, ports, and rivers in the territories of the other, which are or may be opened to foreign commerce, and shall enjoy, respectively, the same treatment in matters of commerce and navigation as native citizens or subjects, or citizens or subjects of the most favoured nation, without having to pay taxes, imposts or duties, of whatever nature or under whatever denomination levied in the name or for the profit of the Government, public functionaries, private individuals, corporations, or establishments of any kind, other or greater than those paid by native citizens or subjects, or citizens or subjects of the most favoured nation.

It is, however, understood that the stipulations contained in this and the preceding Article do not in any way affect the laws, ordinances and regulations with regard to trade, the immigration of labourers, police and public security which are in force or which may hereafter be enacted in either of the two countries.

Article III

The dwellings, manufactories, warehouses, and shops of the citizens or subjects of each of the High Contracting Parties in the territories of the other, and all premises appertaining thereto destined for purposes of residence or commerce, shall be respected.

It shall not be allowable to proceed to make a search of, or a domiciliary visit to, such dwellings and premises, or to examine or inspect books, papers, or accounts, except under the conditions and with the forms prescribed by the laws, ordinances and regulations for citizens or subjects of the country.

ARTICLE IV

No other or higher duties shall be imposed on the importation into the territories of the United States of any article, the produce or manufacture of the territories of His Majesty the Emperor of Japan, from whatever place arriving; and no other or higher duties shall be imposed on the importation into the territories of His Majesty the Emperor of Japan of any article, the produce or manufacture of the territories of the United States, from whatever place arriving, than on the like article produced or manufactured in any other foreign country; nor shall any prohibition be maintained or imposed on the importation of any article, the produce or manufacture of the territories of either of the High Contracting Parties, into the territories of the other, from whatever place arriving, which shall not equally extend to the importation of the like article, being the produce or manufacture of any other country. This last provision is not applicable to the sanitary and other prohibitions occasioned by the necessity of protecting the safety of persons, or of cattle, or of plants useful to agriculture.

ARTICLE V

No other or higher duties or charges shall be imposed in the territories of either of the High Contracting Parties on the exportation of any article to the territories of the other than such as are, or may be, payable on the exportation of the like article to any other foreign country; nor shall any prohibition be imposed on the exportation of any article from the territories of either of the two High Contracting Parties to the territories of the other which shall not equally extend to the exportation of the like article to any other country.

ARTICLE VI

The citizens or subjects of each of the High Contracting Parties shall enjoy in the territories of the other exemption from all transit duties, and a perfect equality of treatment with native citizens or subjects in all that relates to warehousing, bounties, facilities, and drawbacks.

ARTICLE VII

All articles which are or may be legally imported into the ports of the territories of His Majesty the Emperor of Japan in Japanese vessels may likewise be imported into those ports in vessels of the United States, without being liable to any other or higher duties or charges of whatever denomination than if such articles were imported in Japanese vessels; and, reciprocally, all articles which are or may be legally imported into the ports of the territories of the United States in vessels of the United States may likewise be imported into those ports in Japanese vessels, without being liable to any other or higher duties or charges of whatever denomination than if such articles were imported in vessels of the United States. Such reciprocal equality of treatment shall take effect without distinction, whether such articles come directly from the place of origin or from any other place.

In the same manner, there shall be perfect equality of treatment in regard to exportation, so that the same export duties shall be paid, and the same bounties and drawbacks allowed, in the territories of either of the High Contracting Parties on the exportation of any article which is or may be legally exported therefrom, whether such exportation shall take place in Japanese vessels or in vessels of the United States, and whatever may be the place of destination, whether a port of either of the High Contracting Parties or of any third Power.

ARTICLE VIII

No duties of tonnage, harbour, pilotage, lighthouse, quarantine, or other similar or corresponding duties of whatever nature, or under whatever denomination levied in the name or for the profit of Government, public functionaries, private individuals, corporations, or establishments of any kind, shall be imposed in the ports of the territories of either country upon the vessels of the other country which shall not equally and under the same conditions be imposed in the like cases on national vessels in general or vessels of the most favoured nation. Such equality of treatment shall apply reciprocally to the respective vessels, from whatever port or place they may arrive, and whatever may be their place of destination.

ARTICLE IX

In all that regards the stationing, loading, and unloading of vessels in the ports, basins, docks, roadsteads, harbours or rivers of the territories of the two countries, no privilege shall be granted to national vessels which shall not be equally granted to vessels of the other country; the intention of the High Contracting Parties being that in this respect also the respective vessels shall be treated on the footing of perfect equality.

ARTICLE X

The coasting trade of both the High Contracting Parties is excepted from the provisions of the present Treaty, and shall be regulated according to the laws, ordinances and regulations of the United States and Japan, respectively. It is, however, understood that citizens of the United States in the territories of His Majesty the Emperor of Japan and Japanese subjects in the territories of the United States, shall enjoy in this respect the rights which are, or may be, granted under such laws, ordinances and regulations to the citizens or subjects of any other country.

A vessel of the United States laden in a foreign country with cargo destined for two or more ports in the territories of His Majesty the Emperor of Japan, and a Japanese vessel laden in a foreign country with cargo destined for two or more ports in the territories of the United States, may discharge a portion of her cargo at one port, and continue her voyage to the other port or ports of destination where foreign trade is permitted, for the purpose of landing the remainder of her original cargo there, subject always to the laws and customs regulation of the two countries.

The Japanese Government, however, agrees to allow vessels of the United States to continue, as heretofore, for the period of the duration of the present Treaty, to carry cargo between the existing open ports of the Empire, excepting to or from the ports of Osaka, Niigata, and Ebisuminato.

Article XI

Any ship-of-war or merchant vessel of either of the High Contracting Parties which may be compelled by stress of weather, or by reason of any other distress, to take shelter in a port of the other, shall be at liberty to refit therein, to procure all necessary supplies, and to put to sea again, without paying any dues other than such as would be payable by national vessels. In case, however, the master of a merchant vessel should under the necessity of disposing of a part of his cargo in order to defray the expenses, he shall be bound to conform to the regulations and tariffs of the place to which he may have come.

If any ship-of-war or merchant vessel of the High Contracting Parties should run aground or be wrecked upon the coasts of the other, the local authorities shall inform the Consul General, Consul, Vice-Consul, or Consular Agent of the district, of the occurrence, or if there be no such consular officers, they shall inform the Consul General, Consul, Vice-Consul, or Consular Agent of the nearest district.

All proceedings relative to the salvage of Japanese vessels, wrecked or cast on shore in the territorial waters of the United States, shall take place in accordance with the laws of the United States, and, reciprocally, all measures of salvage relative to vessels of the United States, wrecked or cast on shore in the territorial waters of His Majesty the Emperor of Japan, shall take place in accordance with the laws, ordinances, and regulations of Japan.

Such stranded or wrecked ship or vessel, and all parts thereof, and all furniture and appurtenances belonging thereunto, and all goods and merchandise saved therefrom, including those which may have been cast into the sea, or the proceeds thereof, if sold, as well as all papers found on board such stranded or wrecked ship

or vessel, shall be given up to the owners or
their agents, when claimed by them. If such
owners or agents are not on the spot, the same
shall be delivered to the respective Consuls General, Consuls, Vice-Consuls, or Consular Agents
upon being claimed by them within the period
fixed by laws, ordinances and regulations of the
country, and such Consular officers, owners, or
agents shall pay only the expenses incurred in
the preservation of the property, together with
the salvage or other expenses which would have
been payable in the case of the wreck of a
national vessel.

The goods and merchandise saved from the
wreck shall be exempt from all the duties of the
Customs unless cleared for consumption, in
which case they shall pay the ordinary duties.

When a vessel belonging to the citizens or
subjects of one of the High Contracting Parties
is stranded or wrecked in the territories of the
other, the respective Consuls General, Consuls,
Vice-Consuls, and Consular Agents shall be authorized, in case the owner or master, or other
agent of the owner, is not present, to lend their
official assistance in order to afford the necessary assistance to the citizens or subjects of the
respective States. The same rule shall apply in
case the owner, master, or other agent is present, but requires such assistance to be given.

ARTICLE XII

All vessels which, according to United States
law, are to be deemed vessels of the United

States, and all vessels which, according to Japanese law, are to be deemed Japanese vessels, shall, for the purpose of this Treaty, be deemed vessels of the United States and Japanese vessels, respectively.

ARTICLE XIII

The Consuls General, Consuls, Vice-Consuls, and Consular Agents of each of the High Contracting Parties, residing in the territories of the other, shall receive from the local authorities such assistance as can by law be given to them for the recovery of deserters from the vessels of their respective countries.

It is understood that this stipulation shall not apply to the citizens or subjects of the country where the desertion takes place.

ARTICLE XIV

The High Contracting Parties agree that, in all that concerns commerce and navigation, any privilege, favour or immunity which either High Contracting Party has actually granted, or may hereafter grant, to the Government, ships, citizens, or subjects of any other State, shall be extended to the Government, ships, citizens, or subjects of the other High Contracting Party, gratuitously, if the concession in favour of that other State shall have been gratuitous, and on the same or equivalent conditions if the concession shall have been conditional; it being their intention that the trade and navigation of each country shall be placed, in all respects, by the other, upon the footing of the most favoured nation.

ARTICLE XV

Each of the High Contracting Parties may appoint Consuls General, Consuls, Vice-Consuls, Pro-Consuls, and Consular Agents, in all the ports, cities, and places of the other, except in those where it may not be convenient to recognize such officers.

This exception, however, shall not be made in regard to one of the High Contracting Parties without being made likewise in regard to every other Power.

The Consuls General, Consuls, Vice-Consuls, Pro-Consuls, and Consular Agents, may exercise all functions, and shall enjoy all privileges, exemptions, and immunities which are, or may hereafter be granted to Consular officers of the most favoured nation.

ARTICLE XVI

The citizens or subjects of each of the High Contracting Parties shall enjoy in the territories of the other the same protection as native citizens or subjects in regard to patents, trade marks and designs, upon fulfillment of the formalities prescribed by law.

ARTICLE XVII

The High Contracting Parties agree to the following arrangement:

The several Foreign Settlements in Japan shall, from the date this Treaty comes into force, be incorporated with the respective Japanese Communes, and shall thenceforth form part of the general municipal system of Japan. The competent Japanese Authorities shall thereupon assume all municipal obligations and duties in respect thereof, and the common funds and property, if any, belonging to such Settlement shall at the same time be transferred to the said Japanese Authorities.

When such incorporation takes place existing leases in perpetuity upon which property is now held in the said Settlements shall be confirmed, and no conditions whatsoever other than those contained in such existing leases shall be imposed in respect of such property. It is, however, understood that the Consular Authorities mentioned in the same are in all cases to be replaced by the Japanese Authorities. All lands which may previously have been granted by the Japanese Government free of rent for the public purposes of the said Settlement shall, subject to the right of Eminent domain, be permanently reserved free of all taxes and charges for the public purposes for which they were originally set apart.

Article XVIII

This Treaty shall, from the date it comes into force, be substituted in place of the Treaty of Peace and Amity concluded on the 3d day of the 3d month of the 7th year of Kayei, corresponding to the 31st day of March, 1854; the Treaty of Amity and Commerce concluded on the 19th day of the 6th month of the 5th year of Ansei, corresponding to the 29th day of July, 1858; the Tariff Convention concluded on the 13th day of the 5th month of the 2d year of Keio, corresponding to the 25th day of June, 1866; the Convention concluded on the 25th day of the 7th month of the 11th year of Meiji, corresponding to the 25th day of July, 1878, and all Arrangements and Agreements subsidiary thereto concluded or existing between the High Contracting Parties; and from the same date such Treaties, Conventions, Arrangements and Agreements shall cease to be being, and, in consequence, the jurisdiction then exercised by Courts of the United States in Japan and all the exceptional privileges, exemptions and immunities then enjoyed by citizens of the United States as a part of, or appurtenant to such jurisdiction, shall absolutely and without notice cease and determine, and thereafter all such jurisdiction shall be assumed and exercised by Japanese Courts.

ARTICLE XIX

This Treaty shall go into operation on the 17th day of July, 1899, and shall remain in force for the period of twelve years from that date.

Either High Contracting Party shall have the right, at any time thereafter, to give notice to the other of its intention to terminate the same, and at the expiration of twelve months after such notice is given this Treaty shall wholly cease and determine.

ARTICLE XX

This Treaty shall be ratified, and the ratification thereof shall be exchanged, either at Washington or Tokyo, as soon as possible and not later than six months after its signature.

In witness whereof the respective Plenipotentiaries have signed the present Treaty in duplicate and have thereunto affixed their seals.

Done at the City of Washington the 22d day of November, in the eighteen hundred and ninety-fourth year of the Christian era, corresponding to the 22d day of the 11th month of the 27th year of Meiji.

> WALTER Q. GRESHAM   [SEAL].
> SHINICHIRO KURINO   [SEAL].

B

THE EMIGRATION TREATY BETWEEN CHINA AND THE UNITED STATES, 1894

Signed March 17, 1894;
Proclaimed December 8, 1894

Whereas, on the 17th day of November, A. D. 1880, and of Kwanghsu, the sixth year, tenth moon, fifteenth day, a treaty was concluded between the United States and China for the purpose of regulating, limiting, or suspending the coming of Chinese labourers to, and their residence in, the United States;

And, whereas, the Government of China, in view of the antagonism and much deprecated and serious disorders to which the presence of Chinese labourers has given rise in certain parts of the United States, desires to prohibit the emigration of such labourers from China to the United States;

And, whereas, the two Governments desire to coöperate in prohibiting such emigration, and to strengthen in other ways the bonds of friendship between the two countries;

And, whereas, the two Governments are desirous of adopting reciprocal measures for the better protection of the citizens or subjects of each within the jurisdiction of the other;

Now, therefore, the President of the United States has appointed Walter Q. Gresham, Secretary of State of the United States, as his Plenipotentiary, and His Imperial Majesty, the Emperor of China has appointed Yang Yu, Officer of the second rank, Sub-Director of the Court of Sacrificial Worship, and Envoy Extraordinary and Minister Plenipotentiary to the United States of America, as his Plenipotentiary; and the said Plenipotentiaries having exhibited their respective Full Powers found to be in due and good form, have agreed upon the following articles:

ARTICLE I

The High Contracting Parties agree that for

a period of ten years, beginning with the date of
the exchange of the ratifications of this Convention, the coming, except the conditions herein-
after specified, of Chinese labourers to the
United States shall be absolutely prohibited.

ARTICLE II

The preceding Article shall not apply to the
return to the United States of any registered
Chinese labourer who has a lawful wife, child,
or parent in the United States, or property
therein of the value of one thousand dollars, or
debts of like amount due him and pending settlement. Nevertheless every such Chinese labourer shall, before leaving the United States,
deposit, as a condition of his return, with the
collector of customs of the district from which
he departs, a full description in writing of his
family, or property, or debts, as aforesaid, and
shall be furnished by said collector with such
certificate of his right to return under this
Treaty as the laws of the United States may
now or hereafter prescribe and not inconsistent
with the provisions of this Treaty; and should
the written description aforesaid be proved to be
false, the right of return thereunder, or of continued residence after return, shall in each case
be forfeited. And such right of return to the
United States shall be exercised within one year
from the date of leaving the United States; but
such right of return to the United States may be
extended for an additional period, not to exceed
one year, in cases where by reason of sickness or

other cause of disability beyond his control, such Chinese labourer shall be rendered unable sooner to return—which facts shall be fully reported to the Chinese Consul at the port of departure, and by him certified, to the satisfaction of the collector of the port at which such Chinese subject shall land in the United States. And no such Chinese labourer shall be permitted to enter the United States by land or sea without producing to the proper officer of the customs the return certificate herein required.

ARTICLE III

The provisions of this Convention shall not affect the right at present enjoyed of Chinese subjects, being officials, teachers, students, merchants or travellers, for curiosity or pleasure, but not labourers, of coming to the United States and residing therein. To entitle such Chinese subjects as are above described to admission into the United States, they may produce a certificate from their Government or the Government where they last resided viséd by the diplomatic or consular representatives of the United States in the country or port where they depart.

It is also agreed that Chinese labourers shall continue to enjoy the privilege of transit across the territory of the United States in the course of their journey to or from other countries, subject to such regulations by the Government of the United States as may be necessary to prevent said privilege of transit from being abused.

ARTICLE IV

In pursuance of Article III of the Immigration Treaty between the United States and China, signed at Peking on the 17th day of November, 1880 (the 15th day of the tenth month of Kwanghsu, sixth year), it is hereby understood and agreed that Chinese labourers or Chinese of any other class, either permanently or temporarily residing in the United States, shall have for the protection of their persons and property all rights that are given by the laws of the United States to citizens of the most favoured nation, excepting the right to become naturalized citizens. And the Government of the United States reaffirms its obligation, as stated in said Article III, to exert all its power to secure protection to the persons and property of all Chinese subjects in the United States.

ARTICLE V

The Government of the United States, having by an Act of the Congress, approved May 5, 1892, as amended by an Act approved November 3, 1893, required all Chinese labourers lawfully within the limits of the United States before the passage of the first-named Act to be registered as in said Acts provided, with a view of affording them better protection, the Chinese Government will not object to the enforcement of such acts, and reciprocally the Government of the United States recognizes the right of the Government of China to enact and enforce simi-

lar laws or regulations for the registration, free
of charge, of all labourers, skilled or unskilled
(not merchants as defined by said Acts of Congress), citizens of the United States in China,
whether residing within or without the treaty
ports.

And the Government of the United States
agrees that within twelve months from the date
of the exchange of the ratifications of this Convention, and annually, thereafter, it will furnish
to the Government of China registers or reports
showing the full name, age, occupation and
number or place of residence of all other citizens
of the United States, including missionaries, residing both within and without the treaty ports
of China, not including, however, diplomatic
and other officers of the United States residing
or travelling in China upon official business, together with their body and household servants.

ARTICLE VI

This Convention shall remain in force for a
period of ten years beginning with the date of
the exchange of ratifications, and, if six months
before the expiration of the said period of ten
years, neither Government shall have given notice of its final termination to the other, it shall
remain in full force for another like period of
ten years.

In faith whereof, we, the respective plenipotentiaries, have signed this Convention and have
hereunto affixed our seals.

Done, in duplicate, at Washington, the 17th day of March, A. D. 1894.

WALTER Q. GRESHAM   [SEAL].
(CHINESE SIGNATURE)   [SEAL].

C

PROTOCOL BETWEEN CHINA AND THE TREATY POWERS, SEPTEMBER 7, 1901

The plenipotentiaries of Germany, His Excellency M. A. Munn von Schwarzenstein; of Austria-Hungary, His Excellency M. M. Czikann von Wahlborn; of Belgium, His Excellency M. Joostens; of Spain, M. B. J. de Cologan; of the United States, His Excellency M. W. W. Rockhill; of France, His Excellency M. Paul Beau; of Great Britain, His Excellency Sir Ernest Satow; of Italy, Marquis Salvago Raggi; of Japan, His Excellency M. Jutaro Komura; of the Netherlands, His Excellency M. F. M. Knobel; of Russia, His Excellency M. M. deGiers; and of China, His Highness Yi-K'uang Prince Ching of the first rank, President of the Ministry of Foreign Affairs, and His Excellency Li Hung-chang, Earl of Su-i of the first rank, Tutor of the Heir Apparent, Grand Secretary of the Wen-hua Throne Hall, Minister of Commerce, Superintendent of the Northern trade,

Governor-General of Chihli, have met for the purpose of declaring that China has complied to the satisfaction of the Powers with the conditions laid down in the note of the 22d of December, 1900, and which were accepted in their entirety by His Majesty the Emperor of China in a decree dated the 27th of December.

ARTICLE Iᵃ

By an Imperial Edict of the 9th of June last, Tsai Feng, Prince of Ch'un, was appointed Ambassador of His Majesty the Emperor of China, and directed in that capacity to convey to His Majesty the German Emperor the expression of the regrets of His Majesty the Emperor of China and of the Chinese Government for the assassination of His Excellency the late Baron von Ketteler, German Minister.

Prince Ch'un left Peking the 12th of July last to carry out the orders which had been given him.

ARTICLE Iᵇ

The Chinese Government has stated that it will erect on the spot of the assassination of His Excellency the late Baron von Ketteler a commemorative monument, worthy of the rank of the deceased, and bearing an inscription in the Latin, German, and Chinese languages, which shall express the regrets of His Majesty the Emperor of China for the murder committed.

Their Excellencies the Chinese Plenipotentiaries have informed His Excellency the German Plenipotentiary, in a letter dated the 22d of July last, that an arch of the whole width of the street would be erected on the said spot, and that work on it was begun the 25th of June last.

ARTICLE II[a]

Imperial Edicts of the 13th and 21st of February, 1901, inflicted the following punishments on the principal authors of the outrages and crimes committed against the foreign Governments and their nationals:

Tsai-I Prince Tuan and Tsai Lan Duke Fu-kuo were sentenced to be brought before the autumnal court of assize for execution, and it was agreed that if the Emperor saw fit to grant them their lives, they should be exiled to Turkestan and there imprisoned for life, without the possibility of commutation of these punishments.

Tsai Hsun Prince Chuang, Ying Nien, President of the Court of censors, and Chao Shu-Chiao, President of the Board of punishments, were condemned to commit suicide.

Yu Hsien, Governor of Shanhsi, Chi Hsiu, President of the Board of rites, and Hsu Cheng-yu, formerly senior vice-President of the Board of punishments, were condemned to death.

Posthumous degradation was inflicted on Kang Yi, assistant Grand Secretary, President of the Board of works, Hsu Tung, Grand Secretary, and Li Ping-heng, formerly Governor-General of Szu-ch'uan.

An Imperial Edict of February 13th, 1901, rehabilitated the memories of Hsu Yung-yi, President of the Board of War, Li Shan, President of the Board of works, Hsu Ching-cheng, senior vice-President of the Board of works, Lien Yuan, vice-Chancellor of the Grand Council, and Yuan Chang, vice-President of the court of sacrifices, who had been put to death for having protested against the outrageous breaches of international law of last year.

Prince Chuang committed suicide the 21st of February, 1901, Ying Nien and Chao Shu-chiao the 24th, Yu Hsien was executed the 22d, Chi Hsiu and Hsu Cheng-yu on the 26th. Tung Fu-hsiang, General in Kan-su, has been deprived of his office by Imperial Edict of the 13th of February, 1901, pending the determination of the final punishment to be inflicted on him.

Imperial Edicts dated the 29th of April and 19th of August, 1901, have inflicted various punishments on the provincial officials convicted of the crime and outrages of last summer.

ARTICLE II^b

An Imperial Edict promulgated the 19th of August, 1901, ordered the suspension of official examination for five years in all cities where foreigners were massacred or submitted to cruel treatment.

ARTICLE III

So as to make honourable reparation for the assassination of Mr. Sugiyama, chancellor of the Japanese Legation, His Majesty the Emperor of China by an Imperial Edict of the 18th of June, 1901, appointed Na Tung, vice-President of the Board of revenue, to be his Envoy Extraordinary, and specially directed him to convey to His Majesty the Emperor of Japan the expression of the regrets of His Majesty the Emperor of China and of his Government at the assassination of the late Mr. Sugiyama.

Article IV

The Chinese Government has agreed to erect an expiatory monument in each of the foreign or international cemeteries which were desecrated and in which the tombs were destroyed.

It has been agreed with the Representatives of the Powers that the legations interested shall settle the details for the erection of these monuments, China bearing all the expenses thereof, estimated at ten thousand taels for the cemeteries at Peking and within its neighbourhood, and at five thousand taels for the cemeteries in the provinces. The amounts have been paid and the list of these cemeteries is enclosed herewith.

Article V

China has agreed to prohibit the importation into its territory of arms and ammunition, as well as of materials exclusively used for the manufacture of arms and ammunition.

An Imperial Edict has been issued on the 25th of August, 1901, forbidding said importation for a term of two years. New Edict may be issued subsequently extending this by other successive terms of two years in case of necessity recognized by the Powers.

ARTICLE VI

By an Imperial Edict dated the 29th of May, 1901, His Majesty the Emperor of China agreed to pay the Powers an indemnity of four hundred and fifty millions of Haikwan taels. This sum represents the total amount of the indemnities for States, companies or societies, private individuals, and Chinese referred to in Article VI of the note of December 22d, 1900.

(*a*) These four hundred and fifty millions constitute a gold debt calculated at the rate of the Haikwan tael to the gold currency of each country, as indicated below:

```
Haikwan tael—marks ................ 3.055
            —Austria-Hungary crown.. 3.595
            —gold dollar............. 0.742
            —francs ................ 3.750
            —pound sterling......... 3s. od.
            —yen .................. 1.407
            —Netherlands florin....... 1.796
            —gold rouble............ 1.412
```

This sum in gold shall bear interest at 4 per cent. per annum, and the capital shall be reimbursed by China in thirty-nine years in the manner indicated in the annexed plan of amortization.

Capital and interest shall be payable in gold or at the rates of exchange corresponding to the dates at which the different payments fall due.

The amortization shall commence the 1st of January, 1902, and shall finish at the end of the year 1940. The amortizations are payable annually, the first payment being fixed on the 1st of January, 1903.

Interest shall run from the 1st of July, 1901, but the Chinese Government shall have the right to pay off within a term of three years, beginning January, 1902, the arrears of the first six months, ending the 31st of December, 1901, on condition, however, that it pays compound interest at the rate of 4 per cent. per annum on the sums the payments of which shall have thus been deferred. Interest shall be payable semi-annually, the first payment being fixed on the 1st of July, 1902.

(b) The service of the debt shall take place in Shanghai, in the following manner:

Each Power shall be represented by a delegate on a commission of bankers authorized to receive the amount of interest and amortization which shall be paid to it by the Chinese authorities designated for that purpose, to divide it among the interested parties, and to give a receipt for the same.

(c) The Chinese Government shall deliver to the Doyen of the Diplomatic Corps at Peking a bond for the lump sum, which shall subsequently be converted into fractional bonds bearing the signatures of the delegates of the Chinese Government designated for that purpose. This operation and all those relating to issuing of the bonds shall be performed by the above-mentioned Commission, in accordance with the instructions which the Powers shall send their delegates.

(*d*) The proceeds of the revenue assigned to the payment of the bonds shall be paid to the commission.

(*e*) The revenues assigned as security for the bonds are the following:

1. The balance of the revenues of the Imperial maritime Customs after payment of the interest and amortization of preceding loans secured on these revenues, plus the proceeds of the raising to five per cent. effective of the present tariff on maritime imports, including articles until now on the free list, but exempting foreign rice, cereals, and flour, gold and silver bullion and coin.

2. The revenue of the native customs, administered in the open ports by the Imperial maritime Customs.

3. The total revenue of the salt gabelle, exclusive of the fraction previously set aside for other foreign loans.

The raising of the present tariff on imports to five per cent. effective is agreed to on the conditions mentioned below.

It shall be put in force two months after the signing of the present protocol, and no exceptions shall be made except for merchandise shipped not more than ten days after the said signing.

(1) All duties levied on imports " ad valorem " shall be converted as far as possible and

as soon as may be into specific duties. This conversion shall be made in the following manner: The average value of merchandise at the time of their landing during the three years 1897, 1898, and 1899, that is to say, the market price less the amount of import duties and incidental expenses, shall be taken as the basis for the valuation of merchandise. Pending the result of the work of conversion, duties shall be levied " ad valorem."

(2) The beds of the rivers Peiho and Whangpu shall be improved with the financial participation of China.

Article VII

The Chinese Government has agreed that the quarter occupied by the legations shall be considered as one specially reserved for their use and placed under their exclusive control, in which Chinese shall not have the right to reside, and which may be made defensible.

The limits of this quarter have been fixed as follows on the annexed plan:

On the west, the line 1, 2, 3, 4, 5.

On the north, the line 5, 6, 7, 8, 9, 10.

On the east, Ketteler Street (10, 11, 12).

Drawn along the exterior base of the Tartar wall and following the line of the bastions, on the south the line 12.1.

In the protocol annexed to the letter of the 16th of January, 1901, China recognized the right of each Power to maintain a permanent guard in the said quarter for the defense of its legation.

Article VIII

The Chinese Government has consented to raze the forts of Taku and those which might impede free communication between Peking and the sea; steps have been taken for carrying this out.

Article IX

The Chinese Government has conceded the right to the Powers in the protocol annexed to the letter of the 16th of January, 1901, to occupy certain points, to be determined by an agreement between them, for the maintenance of open communication between the capital and the sea. The points occupied by the Powers are:

Huang-tsun, Lang-fang, Yang-tsun, Tientsin, Chun-liang Ch'eng, Tang-ku, Lutai, Tang-shan, Lan-chow, Chang-li, Ch'in-wang tao, Shan-hai kuan.

Article X

The Chinese Government has agreed to post and to have published during two years in all district cities the following Imperial edicts:

(a) Edicts of the 1st of February, prohibiting forever, under pain of death, membership in any anti-foreign society.

(b) Edicts of the 13th and 21st of February, 29th of April, and 19th of August, enumerating the punishments inflicted on the guilty.

(*c*) Edicts of the 19th of August, 1901, pro-hibiting examinations in all cities where foreign-ers were massacred or subjected to cruel treat-ment.

(*d*) Edict of the 1st of February, 1901, declar-ing all governors-general, governors, and pro-vincial or local officials responsible for order in their respective districts, and that in case of new anti-foreign troubles or other infractions of the treaties which shall not be immediately re-pressed, these officials shall immediately be dis-missed, without possibility of being given new functions or new honours.

The posting of these edicts is being carried on throughout the Empire.

ARTICLE XI

The Chinese Government has agreed to nego-tiate the amendments deemed necessary by the foreign Governments to the treaties of com-merce and navigation and the other subjects concerning commercial relations, with the ob-ject of facilitating them.

At present, and as a result of the stipulation contained in Article VI concerning the indem-nity, the Chinese Government agrees to assist in the improvement of the courses of the rivers Peiho and Whangpu, as stated below.

(*a*) The works for the improvement of the navigability of the Peiho, begun in 1898, with the coöperation of the Chinese Government, have been resumed under the direction of an international Commission. As soon as the administration of Tientsin shall have been handed back to the Chinese Government, it will be in a position to be represented on this Commission, and will pay each year a sum of sixty thousand Haikwan taels for maintaining the works.

(b) A conservancy Board, charged with the management and control of the works for straightening the Whangpu and the improvement of the course of that river, is hereby created.

This Board shall consist of members representing the interests of the Chinese Government and those of foreigners in the shipping trade of Shanghai. The expenses incurred for the works and the general management of the undertaking are estimated at the annual sum of four hundred and sixty thousand Haikwan taels for the first twenty years. This sum shall be supplied in equal portions by the Chinese Government and the foreign interests concerned. Detailed stipulations concerning the composition, duties, and revenues of the conservancy Board are embodied in annex hereto.

Article XII

An Imperial Edict of the 24th of July, 1901, reformed the Office of foreign affairs (Tsungli Yamen), on the lines indicated by the Powers, that is to say, transformed it into a Ministry of foreign affairs (Wai-wu Pu), which takes precedence over the six other Ministries of the

State. The same edict appointed the principal members of this Ministry.

An agreement has also been reached concerning the modification of Court ceremonial as regards the reception of foreign Representatives and has been the subject of several notes from the Chinese Plenipotentiaries, the substance of which is embodied in a memorandum herewith annexed.

Finally, it is expressly understood that as regards the declarations specified above and the annexed documents originating with the foreign Plenipotentiaries, the French text only is authoritative.

The Chinese Government having thus complied to the satisfaction of the Powers with the conditions laid down in the above-mentioned note of December 22d, 1900, the Powers have agreed to accede to the wishes of China to terminate the situation created by the disorders of the summer of 1900. In consequence thereof the foreign Plenipotentiaries are authorized to declare in the name of their Governments that, with the exception of the legation guards mentioned in Article VII, the international troops will completely evacuate the city of Peking on the 17th of September, 1901, and, with the exception of the localities mentioned in Article IX, will withdraw from the province of Chihli on the 22d of September.

The present final Protocol has been drawn up in twelve identic copies and signed by all the Plenipotentiaries of the Contracting Countries.

One copy shall be given to each of the foreign Plenipotentiaries, and one copy shall be given to the Chinese Plenipotentiaries.

Peking, 7th September, 1901.

A. V. MUMM.	ERNEST SATOW.	*Signatures*
M. CZIKANN.	SALVAGO RAGGI.	*and*
JOOSTENS.	JUTARO KOMURA.	*seals of*
B. J. DE COLOGAN.	F. M. KNOBEL.	*Chinese*
W. W. ROCKHILL.	M. DE GIERS.	*Plenipoten-*
BEAU.		*tiaries.*

D

THE HAY DOCTRINE: THE HAY-VON BÜLOW CORRESPONDENCE

Mr. Hay, American Secretary of State, to Mr. White, American Ambassador to Germany:

Department of State,
Washington, September 6, 1899.

SIR:

At the time when the Government of the United States was informed by that of Germany that it had leased from His Majesty the Emperor of China the port of Kiaochow and the adjacent territory in the province of Shantung, assurances were given to the Ambassador of the United States at Berlin by the Imperial German Minister for Foreign Affairs that the rights and privileges insured by treaties with China to citizens of the United States would not thereby suffer or be in any wise impaired within the area over which Germany had thus obtained control.

More recently, however, the British Government recognized by a formal agreement with Germany the exclusive right of the latter country to enjoy in said leased area and the contiguous "sphere of influence or interest" certain privileges, more especially those relating to railroads and mining enterprises; but, as the exact nature and extent of the rights thus recognized have not been clearly defined, it is possible that serious conflicts of interests may at any time arise, not only between British and German subjects within said area, but that the interests of our citizens may also be jeopardized thereby.

Earnestly desirous to remove any cause of irritation and to insure at the same time to the commerce of all nations in China the undoubted benefits which should accrue from a formal recognition by the various Powers claiming "spheres of interest" that they shall enjoy perfect equality of treatment for their commerce and navigation within such "spheres," the Government of the United States would be pleased to see His German Majesty's Government give formal assurances, and lend its coöperation in securing like assurances from the other interested Powers, that each within its respective sphere of whatever influence—

First. Will in no way interfere with any treaty port or any vested interest within any so-called "sphere of interest" or leased territory it may have in China.

Second.   That the Chinese treaty tariff of the
time being shall apply to all merchandise landed
or shipped to all such ports as are within said
" sphere of interest " (they be " free ports "),
no matter to what nationality it may belong,
and that duties so leviable shall be collected by
the Chinese Government.

Third.   That it will levy no higher dues on
vessels of another nationality frequenting any
port in such " sphere " than shall be levied on
vessels of its own nationality, and no higher railroad charges over lines built, controlled, or op-
erated within its " sphere " on merchandise belonging to citizens or subjects of other nationali-
ties transported through such " sphere " than
shall be levied on similar merchandise belonging
to its own nationals transported over equal dis-
tances.

The liberal policy pursued by His Imperial
German Majesty in declaring Kiaochow a free
port and in aiding the Chinese Government in
the establishment there of a custom-house are
so clearly in line with the proposition which this
Government is anxious to see recognized that
it entertains the strongest hope that Germany
will give its acceptance and hearty support.

The recent Ukase of His Majesty the Emperor of Russia declaring the port of Ta-lien-
wan open during the whole of the lease under
which it is held from China to the merchant
ships of all nations, coupled with the categorical
assurances made to this Government by His Imperial Majesty's representative at this capital at

the time, and since repeated to me by the present Russian Ambassador, seem to insure support of the Emperor to the proposal measure. Our Ambassador at the Court of St. Petersburg has in consequence been instructed to submit it to the Russian Government and to request their early consideration of it. A copy of my instruction on the subject to Mr. Tower is herewith enclosed for your confidential information.

The commercial interests of Great Britain and Japan will be so clearly served by the desired declaration of intentions, and the views of the Governments of these countries as to the desirability of the adoption of measures insuring the benefits of equality of treatment of all foreign trade throughout China are so similar to those entertained by the United States, that their acceptance of the proposition herein outlined and their coöperation in advocating their adoption by the other Powers can be confidently expected. I enclose herewith copy of the instruction which I have sent to Mr. Choate on the subject.

In view of the present favourable conditions, you are instructed to submit the above considerations to His Imperial German Majesty's Minister for Foreign Affairs, and to request his early consideration of the subject.

Copy of this instruction is sent to our Ambassadors at London and at St. Petersburg for their information.

I have, etc.

JOHN HAY.

Count von Bülow, His Imperial German Majesty's Minister for Foreign Affairs, to Mr. White:

(*Translation.*)

Foreign Office,
Berlin, February 19, 1900.

MR. AMBASSADOR:

Your Excellency informed me, in a memorandum presented on the 24th of last month, that the Government of the United States of America had received satisfactory replies from all the Powers to which an inquiry had been addressed similar to that contained in Your Excellency's note of September 26th last, in regard to the policy of the open door in China. While referring to this, Your Excellency thereupon expressed the wish that the Imperial Government would now also give its answer in writing.

Gladly complying with this wish, I have the honour to inform Your Excellency, repeating the statements already made verbally, as follows: As recognized by the Government of the United States of America, according to Your Excellency's note referred to above, the Imperial Government has, from the beginning, not only asserted, but also practically carried out to the fullest extent in its Chinese possessions absolute equality of treatment of all nations with regard to trade, navigation, and commerce. The Imperial Government entertains no thought of departing in the future from this principle, which at once excludes any prejudicial or disadvantageous commercial treatment of the citizens of the United States of America, so long as it is not forced to do so, on account of considerations of reciprocity, by a divergence from it by other governments. If, therefore, the other Powers interested in the industrial development of the Chinese Empire are willing to recognize the same principle, this can only be desired by the Imperial Government, which in this case upon being requested will gladly be ready to participate with the United States of America and the other Powers in an agreement made upon these lines, by which the same rights are reciprocally secured.

I avail myself, etc.

BÜLOW.

E

THE ANGLO-JAPANESE ALLIANCES

(*1st*) *Agreement, Concluded January 30, 1902*

Article I.—The High Contracting Parties, having mutually recognized the independence of China and Korea, declare themselves to be entirely uninfluenced by any aggressive tendencies in either country. Having in view, however, their special interests, of which those of Great Britain relate principally to China, while Japan, in addition to the interests which she possesses in China, is interested in a peculiar degree politically, as well as commercially and industrially, in Korea, the High Contracting Parties recognize that it will be admissible for either of them to take such measures as may be indispensable in order to safeguard those interests if threatened either by the aggressive action of any other Power, or by disturbances arising in China or Korea, and necessitating the intervention of either of the High Contracting Parties for the protection of the lives and property of its subjects.

Article II.—If either Great Britain or Japan, in the defense of their respective interests as above described, should become involved in war with another Power, the other High Contracting Party will maintain a strict neutrality, and use its efforts to prevent others from joining in hostilities against its ally.

Article III.—If, in the above event, any other Power or Powers should join in hostilities against that Ally, the other High Contracting Party will come to its assistance, and will conduct the war in common, and will make peace in mutual agreement with it.

Article IV.—The High Contracting Parties agree that neither of them will, without consulting the other, enter into separate arrangements with another Power to the prejudice of the interests above described.

Article V.—Whenever, in the opinion of either Great Britain or Japan, the above-mentioned interests are in jeopardy the two Governments will communicate with each other fully and frankly.

Article VI.—The present Agreement shall come into effect immediately after the date of its signature, and remain in force for five years from that date. In case neither of the High Contracting Parties should have notified twelve months before the expiration of the said five years the intention of terminating it, it shall remain binding until the expiration of one year from the day on which either of the High Contracting Parties shall have denounced it. But if, when the date fixed for its expiration arrives, either ally is actually engaged in war, the Alliance shall, *ipso facto*, continue until peace is concluded.

(*2d*) *Signed at London August 12, 1905*
The Marquess of Lansdowne to Sir C. Hardinge:

Foreign Office, September 6, 1905.

Sir:

I inclose, for your Excellency's information, a copy of a new Agreement concluded between His Majesty's Government and that of Japan in substitution for that of the 30th of January, 1902. You will take an early opportunity of communicating the new Agreement to the Russian Government.

It was signed on the 12th August, and you will explain that it would have been immediately made public but for the fact that negotiations had at that time already commenced between Russia and Japan, and that the publication of such a document whilst those negotiations were still in progress would obviously have been improper and inopportune.

The Russian Government will, I trust, recognize that the new Agreement is an international instrument to which no exception can be taken by any of the Powers interested in the affairs of the Far East. You should call special attention to the objects mentioned in the preamble as those by which the policy of the Contracting Parties is inspired. His Majesty's Government believed that they may count upon the good will and support of all the Powers in endeavouring to maintain peace in Eastern Asia and in seeking to uphold the integrity and independence of the Chinese Empire and the principle of equal opportunities for the commerce and industry of all nations in that country.

On the other hand, the special interests of the Contracting Parties are of a kind upon which they are fully entitled to insist, and the announcement that those interests must be safeguarded is one which can create no surprise, and need give rise to no misgivings.

I call your special attention to the wording of Article II, which lays down distinctly that it is only in the case of an unprovoked attack made on one of the Contracting Parties by another Power or Powers, and when that Party is defending its territorial rights and special interests from aggressive action, that the other Party is bound to come to its assistance.

Article III, dealing with the question of Korea, is deserving of special attention. It recognizes in the clearest terms the paramount position which Japan at this moment occupies and must henceforth occupy in Korea, and her right to take any measures which she may find necessary for the protection of her political, military, and economic interests in that country. It is, however, expressly provided that such measures must not be contrary to the principle of equal opportunities for the commerce and industry of other nations. The new treaty no doubt differs at this point conspicuously from that of 1902. It has, however, become evident that Korea, owing to its close proximity to the Japanese Empire and inability to stand alone, must fall under the control and tutelage of Japan.

His Majesty's Government observe with satisfaction that this point was readily conceded by Russia in the Treaty of Peace recently concluded with Japan, and they have every reason to believe that similar views are held by other Powers with regard to the relations which should subsist between Japan and Korea.

His Majesty's Government venture to anticipate that the alliance thus concluded, designated as it is with objects which are purely peaceful and for the protection of rights and interests the validity of which cannot be contested, will be regarded with approval by the Government to which you are accredited. They are justified in believing that its conclusion may not have been without effect in facilitating the settlement by which the war has been so happily brought to an end, and they earnestly trust that it may, for many years to come, be instrumental in securing the peace of the world in those regions which come within its scope.

I am, etc.

(Signed)   LANDSDOWNE.,

(Inclosure.)

AGREEMENT BETWEEN THE UNITED KINGDOM AND JAPAN

Signed at London, August 12, 1905

(*Preamble*)

The Governments of Great Britain and Japan, being desirous of replacing the Agreement concluded between them on the 30th January, 1902, by fresh stipulations, have agreed upon the following Articles which have for their objects:

(*a*) The consolidation and maintenance of the general peace in the regions of Eastern Asia and of India;

(*b*) The preservation of the common interest of all Powers in China by insuring the independence and integrity of the Chinese Empire and the principle of equal opportunities for the commerce and industry of all nations in China;

(*c*) The maintenance of the territorial rights of the High Contracting Parties in the regions of Eastern Asia and of India, and the defense of their special interests in the said regions:

Article I.—It is agreed that whenever, in the opinion of either Great Britain or Japan, any of the rights and interests referred to in the preamble of this Agreement are in jeopardy, the two Governments will communicate with one another fully and frankly, and will consider in common the measures which should be taken to safeguard those menaced rights or interests.

Article II.—If by reason of unprovoked attack or aggressive action, wherever arising, on the part of any other Power or Powers either Contracting Party should be involved in war in defense of its territorial rights or special interests mentioned in the preamble of this Agreement, the other Contracting Party will at once come to the assistance of its ally, and will conduct the war in common, and make peace in mutual agreement with it.

Article III.—Japan possessing paramount political, military and economic interests in Korea, Great Britain recognizes the right of Japan to take such measures of guidance, control, and protection in Korea as she may deem proper and necessary to safeguard and advance those interests, provided always that such measures are not contrary to the principle of equal opportunities for the commerce and industry of all nations.

Article IV.—Great Britain having a special interest in all that concerns the security of the Indian frontier, Japan recognizes her right to take such measures in the proximity of that frontier as she may find necessary for safeguarding her Indian possessions.

Article V.—The High Contracting Parties agree that neither of them will, without consulting the other, enter into separate arrangements with another Power to the prejudice of the objects described in the preamble of this Agreement.

Article VI.—As regards the present war between Japan and Russia, Great Britain will continue to maintain strict neutrality unless some other Power or Powers should join in hostilities against Japan, in which case Great Britain will come to the assistance of Japan, and will conduct the war in common, and make peace in mutual agreement with Japan.

Article VII.—The conditions under which armed assistance shall be afforded by either Power to the other in the circumstances mentioned in the present Agreement, and the means by which such assistance is to be made available, will be arranged by the Naval and Military authorities of the Contracting Parties, who will from time to time consult one another fully and freely upon all questions of mutual interest.

Article VIII.—The present Agreement shall, subject to the provisions of Article VI, come into effect immediately after the date of its signature, and remain in force for ten years from that date.

In case neither of the High Contracting Parties should have notified twelve months before the expiration of the said ten years the in-

tention of terminating it, it shall remain binding until the expiration of one year from the
day on which either of the High Contracting
Parties shall have denounced it. But if, when
the date fixed for its expiration arrives, either
ally is actually engaged in war, the alliance
shall, *ipso facto*, continue until peace is concluded.

In faith whereof the Undersigned, duly
authorized by their respective Governments,
have signed this Agreement and have affixed
thereto their Seals.

Done in duplicate at London, the 12th day
of August, 1905.

(L. S.)   LANDSDOWNE,
*His Britannic Majesty's Principal Secretary of State
for Foreign Affairs.*

(L. S.)   TADASU HAYASHI,
*Envoy Extraordinary and Minister Plenipotentiary of
His Majesty the Emperor of Japan at the Court
of St. James.*

(*3d*) *Alliance Treaty Signed July 13, 1911*
(*Preamble*)

The Government of Japan and the Government of Great Britain having in view the important changes which have taken place in the
situation since the conclusion of the Anglo-
Japanese Agreement of August 12, 1905, and
believing that the revision of that Agreement

responding to such changes would contribute to general stability and repose, have agreed upon the following stipulations to replace the Agreement above mentioned, such stipulations having the same object as the said Agreement, namely:—

A.—The consolidation and maintenance of the general peace in the regions of Eastern Asia and India.

B.—The preservation of the common interests of all the Powers in China by insuring the independence and integrity of the Chinese Empire and the principle of equal opportunities for the commerce and industry of all nations in China.

C.—The maintenance of the territorial rights of the High Contracting Parties in the regions of Eastern Asia and of India and the defense of their special interests on those regions:—

Article I.—It is agreed that whenever, in the opinion of either Japan or Great Britain, any of the rights and interests referred to in the preamble of this Agreement are in jeopardy, the two Governments will communicate with one another fully and frankly, and will consider in common the measures which should be taken to safeguard those menaced rights and interests.

Article II.—If by reason of an unprovoked attack or aggressive action, wherever arising, on the part of any other Power or Powers, either of the High Contracting Parties should be involved in war in defense of its territorial rights or special interests mentioned in the preamble

of this Agreement, the other High Contracting
Party will at once come to the assistance of its
ally and will conduct the war in common and
make peace in mutual agreement with it.

Article III.—The High Contracting Parties
agree that neither of them will, without consulting the other, enter into a separate agreement with another Power to the prejudice of
the objects described in the preamble of this
Agreement.

Article IV.—Should either of the High Contracting Parties conclude a treaty of general
arbitration with a third Power, it is agreed that
nothing in this Agreement shall impose on such
contracting party an obligation to go to war
with the Power with whom such an arbitration
treaty is in force.

Article V.—The conditions under which armed
assistance shall be afforded by either Power to
the other in circumstances entered into the
present Agreement, and the means by which
such assistance is to be made available, will be
arranged by the military and naval authorities
of the High Contracting Parties, who will from
time to time consult one another fully and
frankly upon all questions of mutual interests.

Article VI.—The present Agreement shall
come into effect immediately after the date of
its signature, and remain in force for ten years
from that date (same proviso as first Agreement as to expiry).

In faith whereof the undersigned, duly
authorized by their respective Governments,

have signed this Agreement and have affixed their seals thereto.

Done at London, July 13, 1911.

T. KATO,
The Ambassador of His Majesty the Emperor of Japan at the Court of St. James.

EDWARD GREY,
H. B. M.'s Secretary of State for Foreign Affairs.

F

SENATE RESOLUTION 103
64th Congress, 1st Session
IN THE SENATE OF THE UNITED STATES
February 21, 1916

Mr. Stone submitted the following resolution, which was considered and agreed to.[1]

RESOLUTION

Resolved, That the President be requested, if not incompatible with the public interests, to transmit to the Senate the correspondence, or so much thereof as in his opinion may be made public, had between the official representatives of the Government of the United States and the representatives of the Government of Korea re-

[1] Senator Stone of Missouri was the Chairman of the Committee on Foreign Relations.

lating to the occupation of Korea and the establishment of a protectorate over said country by Japan during, or as an incident of, the Russian-Japanese War of nineteen hundred and four and nineteen hundred and five.

G

MESSAGE FROM THE PRESIDENT OF THE UNITED STATES

To the Senate:

In response to the resolution adopted by the Senate on February 21, 1916, requesting the President, if not incompatible with the public interests, to transmit to the Senate the correspondence, or so much thereof as in his opinion may be made public, had between the official representatives of the Government of the United States and the representatives of the Government of Korea, relating to the occupation of Korea and the establishment of a protectorate over said country by Japan, during, or as an incident of, the Russian-Japanese War of 1904–05, I transmit herewith a report by the Secretary of State on this subject.

The report of the Secretary of State has my approval.

WOODROW WILSON.

The White House,
Washington, February 23, 1916.

H

TREATY BETWEEN THE UNITED STATES AND COREA

Peace, Amity, Commerce, and Navigation

Signed at Yin-Chuen (Gensan), May 22, 1882.
Ratification advised by the Senate, January 9, 1883.
Ratified by the President, February 13, 1883.
Ratifications exchanged at Seoul, May 19, 1883.
Proclaimed, June 4, 1883.

BY THE PRESIDENT OF THE UNITED STATES OF AMERICA

A PROCLAMATION

Whereas a treaty of peace and amity and commerce and navigation between the United States of America and the Kingdom of Corea or Chosen was concluded on the twenty-second day of May, one thousand eight hundred and eighty-two, the original of which treaty being in the English and Chinese languages is word for word as follows:

TREATY BETWEEN THE UNITED STATES OF AMERICA AND THE KINGDOM OF CHOSEN

The United States of America and the King-dom of Chosen, being sincerely desirous of establishing permanent relations of amity and friendship between their respective peoples, have to this end appointed—that is to say, the President of the United States—R. W. Shufeldt, Commodore U. S. Navy, as his Commissioner Plenipotentiary, and His Majesty, the King of Chosen, Shin-Chen, President of the Royal Cabinet, Chin-Hong-Chi, member of the Royal Cabinet, as his Commissioners Plenipotentiary, who, having reciprocally examined their respective full powers, which have been found to be in due form, have agreed upon the several following articles:

Article I.—There shall be perpetual peace and friendship between the President of the United States and the King of Chosen and the citizens and subjects of their respective Governments.

If other Powers deal unjustly or oppressively with either Government, the other will exert their good offices, on being informed of the case, to bring about an amicable arrangement, thus showing their friendly feelings.

Article II.—After the conclusion of this Treaty of amity, and commerce, the High Contracting Powers may each appoint Diplomatic Representatives to reside at the Court of the other, and may each appoint Consular Representatives at the ports of the other, which are open to foreign commerce, at their own convenience.

These officials shall have relations with the corresponding local authorities of equal rank upon a basis of mutual equality.

The Diplomatic and Consular Representatives of the two Governments shall receive mutually all the privileges, rights and immunities without discrimination, which are accorded to the same classes of Representatives from the most favoured nation.

Consuls shall exercise their functions only on receipt of an *exequatur* from the Government, to which they are accredited. Consular authorities shall be *bona fide* officials. No merchants shall be permitted to exercise the duties of the office, nor shall Consular officers be allowed to engage in trade. All ports, to which no Consular Representatives have been appointed, the Consuls of other Powers may be invited to act, provided that no merchant shall be allowed to assume Consular functions, or the provisions of this Treaty may, in such cases, be enforced by the local authorities.

If Consular Representatives of the United States in Chosen conduct their business in an improper manner, their *exequatur* may be revoked, subject to the approval previously obtained of the Diplomatic Representative of the United States.

Article III.—Whenever United States vessels, either because of stress of weather, or by want of fuel or provisions, cannot reach the nearest open port in Chosen, they may enter any port or harbour, either to take refuge therein, or to get supplies of wood, coal and other necessaries, or to make repairs, the expenses incurred thereby being defrayed by the ship's master. In such event the officers and people of the locality shall display their sympathy by rendering full assistance, and their liberality by furnishing the necessities required.

If a United States vessel carries on a clandestine trade at a port not open to foreign commerce, such vessel with her cargo shall be seized and confiscated.

If a United States vessel be wrecked on the coast of Chosen, the local authorities, on being informed of the occurrence, shall immediately render assistance to the crew, provide for their present necessities, and take the measures necessary for the salvage of the ship and the preservation of her cargo. They shall also bring the matter to the knowledge of the nearest Consular Representative of the United States, in order that steps may be taken to send the crew home and to save the ship and cargo. The necessary expenses shall be defrayed either by the ship's master or by the United States.

Article IV.—All citizens of the United States of America in Chosen, peaceably attending to their own affairs, shall receive and enjoy for themselves and everything appertaining to them, the protection of the local authorities of the Government of Chosen, who shall defend them from all insult and injury of any sort. If their dwellings or property be threatened or attacked by mobs, incendiaries, or other violent or lawless persons, the local officers, on requisition of the Consul, shall immediately dispatch a military force to disperse the rioters, apprehend the guilty individuals, and punish them with the utmost rigour of the law. Subjects of

Chosen, guilty of any criminal act toward citizens of the United States, shall be punished by the authorities of Chosen according to the laws of Chosen; and citizens of the United States, either on shore or in any merchant-vessel, who may insult, trouble or wound the persons or injure the property of the people of Chosen, shall be arrested and punished only by the Consul or other public functionary of the United States thereto authorized, according to the laws of the United States.

When controversies arise in the Kingdom of Chosen between citizens of the United States and subjects of His Majesty, which need to be examined and decided by the public officers of the two nations, it is agreed between the two Governments of the United States and Chosen that such cases shall be tried by the proper official of the nationality of the defendant, according to the laws of that nation.

The properly authorized official of the plaintiff's nationality shall be freely permitted to attend the trial, and shall be treated with the courtesy due to his position. He shall be granted all proper facilities for watching the proceedings in the interests of justice. If he so desires, he shall have the right to be present, to examine and to cross-examine witnesses. If he is dissatisfied with the proceedings, he shall be permitted to protest against them in detail.

It is, however, mutually agreed and understood between the High Contracting Powers that whenever the King of Chosen shall have so far modified and reformed the statutes and judicial procedure of his Kingdom that, in the judgment of the United States, they conform to the laws and course of justice in the United States, the right of exterritorial jurisdiction over United States citizens in Chosen shall be abandoned, and thereafter United States citizens, when within the limits of the Kingdom of Chosen, shall be subject to the jurisdiction of the native authorities.

Article V.—Merchants and merchant-vessels of Chosen visiting the United States for purposes of traffic, shall pay duties and tonnage dues and all fees according to the Customs Regulations of the United States, but no higher or other rates of duties and tonnage dues shall be exacted of them than are levied upon citizens of the United States or upon citizens or subjects of the most favoured nation.

Merchants and merchant-vessels of the United States visiting Chosen for purposes of traffic shall pay duties upon all merchandise imported and exported. The authority to levy duties is of right vested in the Government of Chosen. The tariff of duties upon exports and imports, together with the Customs Regulations for the prevention of smuggling and other irregularities, will be fixed by the authorities of Chosen and communicated to the proper officials of the United States, to be by the latter notified to their citizens and duly observed. It is, however, agreed in the first instance, as a general measure, that the tariff upon such imports as are articles of daily use shall not exceed an *ad valorem* duty of ten per centum; that the tariff upon such imports as are luxuries, as, for instance, foreign wines, foreign tobacco, clocks and watches, shall not exceed an *ad valorem* duty of thirty per centum, and that native produce exported shall pay a duty not to exceed five per centum *ad valorem*. And it is further agreed that the duty upon foreign imports shall be paid once for all at the port of entry, and that no other dues, duties, fees, taxes, or charges of any sort shall be levied upon such imports either in the interior of Chosen or at the ports.

United States merchant-vessels entering the ports of Chosen shall pay tonnage dues at the rate of five mace per ton, payable once in three months on each vessel, according to the Chinese calendar.

Article VI.—Subjects of Chosen who may visit the United States shall be permitted to reside and to rent premises, purchase land, or to construct residences or warehouses in all parts of the country. They shall be freely permitted to pursue their various callings and avocations, and to traffic in all merchandise, raw and manufactured, that is not declared contraband by law.

Citizens of the United States who may resort to the ports of Chosen which are open to foreign commerce, shall be permitted to reside at such open ports within the limits of the concessions and to lease buildings or land, or to construct residences or warehouses therein. They shall be freely permitted to pursue their

various callings and avocations within the limits
of the port, and to traffic in all merchandise, raw
and manufactured, that is not declared contraband by law.

No coercion or intimidation in the acquisition of land or buildings shall be permitted, and
the land-rent as fixed by the authorities of
Chosen shall be paid. And it is expressly
agreed that land so acquired in the open ports
of Chosen still remain an integral part of the
Kingdom, and that all rights of jurisdiction over
persons and property within such areas remain
vested in the authorities of Chosen, except in
so far as such rights have been expressly re-
linquished by this Treaty.

American citizens are not permitted either to
transport foreign imports to the interior for
sale, or to proceed thither to purchase native
produce. Nor are they permitted to transport
native produce from one open port to another
open port.

Violation of this rule will subject such merchandise to confiscation, and the merchants offending will be handed over to the Consular
Authorities to be dealt with.

Article VII.—The Governments of the United
States and of Chosen mutually agree and undertake that subjects of Chosen shall not be permitted to import opium into any of the ports
of the United States, and citizens of the United
States shall not be permitted to import opium
into any of the open ports of Chosen, to transport it from one open port to another open port,

or to traffic in it in Chosen.   This absolute prohibition which extends to vessels owned by the
citizens or subjects of either Power, to foreign
vessels employed by them, and to vessels owned
by the citizens or subjects of either Power and
employed by other persons for the transportation of opium, shall be enforced by appropriate
legislation on the part of the United States and
of Chosen, and offenders against it shall be
severely punished.

Article VIII.—Whenever the Government of
Chosen shall have reason to apprehend a
scarcity of food within the limits of the Kingdom, His Majesty may by Decree temporarily
prohibit the export of all breadstuffs, and such
Decree shall be binding on all citizens of the
United States in Chosen upon due notice having
been given them by the Authorities of Chosen
through the proper officers of the United States;
but it is to be understood that the exportation
of rice and breadstuffs of every description is
prohibited from the open port of Yin-Chuen.

Chosen having of old prohibited the exportation of red-ginseng, if citizens of the United
States clandestinely purchase it for export, it
shall be confiscated and the offenders punished.

Article IX.—The purchase of cannon, small
arms, swords, gunpowder, shot and all munitions of war is permitted only to officials of the
Government of Chosen, and they may be imported by citizens of the United States only under a written permit from the authorities of
Chosen.   If these articles are clandestinely im-

ported, they shall be confiscated and the offending parties shall be punished.

Article X.—The officers and people of either nation residing in the other shall have the right to employ natives for all kinds of lawful work.

Should, however, subjects of Chosen, guilty of violations of the laws of the Kingdom, or against whom any action has been brought, conceal themselves in the residences or warehouses of United States citizens, or on board United States merchant-vessels, the Consular Authorities of the United States, on being informed of the fact by the local authorities, will either permit the latter to dispatch constables to make the arrests, or the persons will be arrested by the Consular Authorities and handed over to the local constables.

Officials or citizens of the United States shall not harbour such persons.

Article XI.—Students of either nationality who may proceed to the country of the other, in order to study the language, literature, laws or arts shall be given all possible protection and assistance in evidence of cordial good will.

Article XII.—This, being the first Treaty negotiated by Chosen, and hence being general and incomplete in its provisions, shall in the first instance be put into operation in all things stipulated herein. As to stipulations not contained herein, after an interval of five years, when the officers and people of the two Powers shall have become more familiar with each other's language, a further negotiation of commercial provisions and regulations in detail, in conformity with international law and without unequal discrimination on either part shall be had.

Article XIII.—This Treaty, and future official correspondence between the two contracting Governments shall be made, on the part of Chosen, in the Chinese language.

The United States shall either use the Chinese language, or, if English be used, it shall be accompanied with a Chinese version, in order to avoid misunderstanding.

Article XIV.—The High Contracting Powers hereby agree that, should at any time the King of Chosen grant to any nation or to the merchants or citizens of any nation any right, privilege or favour, connected either with navigation, commerce, political or other intercourse, which is not conferred by this Treaty, such right, privilege and favour shall freely inure to the benefit of the United States, its public officers, merchants and citizens, provided always that whenever such right, privilege or favour is accompanied by any condition, or equivalent concession granted by the other nation interested, the United States, its officers and people shall only be entitled to the benefits of such right, privilege or favour upon complying with the conditions or concessions connected therewith.

In faith whereof the respective Commissioners Plenipotentiary have signed and sealed the foregoing at Yin-Chuen in English and

Chinese, being three originals of each test of
even tenor and date, the ratifications of which
shall be exchanged at Yin-Chuen within one
year from the date of its execution, and immediately thereafter this Treaty shall be in all its
provisions publicly proclaimed and made known
by both Governments in their respective countries, in order that it may be obeyed by their
citizens and subjects respectively.

Chosen, May, the 22nd, A. D. 1882.

[SEAL]   R. W. SHUFELDT, Commodore, U. S. N.
Envoy of the U. S. to Chosen.

[SEAL]   SHIN CHEN,   CHIN HONG CHI,
Members of the Royal Cabinet of Chosen.

And whereas the Senate of the United States
of America by their resolution of the ninth of
January, one thousand eight hundred and
eighty-three (two-thirds of the Senators present
concurring), did advise and consent to the ratification of said treaty subject to the condition
following, viz:

Resolved, That it is the understanding of the
Senate in agreeing to the foregoing resolution,
that the clause, " Nor are they permitted to
transport native produce from one open port to
another open port," in Article VI of said treaty,
is not intended to prohibit and does not prohibit
American ships from going from one open port
to another open port in Corea or Chosen to
receive Corean cargo for exportation, or to discharge foreign cargo.

And whereas, said treaty has been duly ratified on both parts, subject to said condition, and the respective ratifications thereof exchanged.

Now, therefore, be it known that I, Chester A. Arthur, President of the United States of America, have caused the said convention to be made public, to the end that the same, and every clause and article thereof, may be observed and fulfilled with good faith by the United States and the citizens thereof.

In witness whereof I have hereunto set my hand and caused the seal of the United States to be affixed.

Done at the city of Washington this Fourth day of June, in the year of our Lord one thousand eight hundred and eighty-three and of the Independence of the United States of America the one hundredth and seventh.

CHESTER A. ARTHUR.

By the President.
FREDK. T. FRELINGHUYSEN,
Secretary of State.

I

PETITION FROM THE KOREANS OF HAWAII TO PRESIDENT ROOSEVELT

Honolulu, T. H.,
July 12, 1905.

TO HIS EXCELLENCY,
The President of the United States.
Your Excellency,—The undersigned have

been authorized by the 8,000 Koreans now residing in the territory of Hawaii at a special mass meeting held in the city of Honolulu, on July 12, 1905, to present to your Excellency the following appeal:—

We, the Koreans of the Hawaiian Islands, voicing the sentiments of twelve millions of our countrymen, humbly lay before your Excellency the following facts:—

Soon after the commencement of the war between Russia and Japan, our Government made a treaty of alliance with Japan for offensive and defensive purposes. By virtue of this treaty the whole of Korea was opened to the Japanese, and both the Government and the people have been assisting the Japanese authorities in their military operations in and about Korea.

The contents of this treaty are undoubtedly known to your Excellency, therefore we need not embody them in this appeal. Suffice it to state, however, the object of the treaty was to preserve the independence of Korea and Japan and to protect Eastern Asia from Russia's aggression.

Korea, in return for Japan's friendship and protection against Russia, has rendered services to the Japanese by permitting them to use the country as a base of their military operations.

When this treaty was concluded, the Koreans fully expected that Japan would introduce reforms into the governmental administration along the line of the modern civilization of

Europe and America, and that she would advise and counsel our people in a friendly manner, but to our disappointment and regret the Japanese Government has not done a single thing in the way of improving the condition of the Korean people. On the contrary, she turned loose several thousand rough and disorderly men of her nationals in Korea, who are treating the inoffensive Koreans in a most outrageous manner. The Koreans are by nature not a quarrelsome or aggressive people, but deeply resent the high-handed action of the Japanese toward them. We can scarcely believe that the Japanese Government approves the outrages committed by its people in Korea, but it has done nothing to prevent this state of affairs. They have been, during the last eighteen months, forcibly obtaining all the special privileges and concessions from our Government, so that to-day they practically own everything that is worth having in Korea.

We, the common people of Korea, have lost confidence in the promises Japan made at the time of concluding the treaty of alliance, and we doubt seriously the good intentions which she professes to have toward our people. For geographical, racial, and commercial reasons we want to be friendly to Japan, and we are even willing to have her as our guide and example in the matters of internal reforms and education, but the continuous policy of self-exploitation at the expense of the Koreans has shaken our confidence in her, and we are now afraid that she will not keep her promise of preserving our independence as a nation, nor assisting us in reforming internal administration. In other words, her policy in Korea seems to be exactly the same as that of Russia prior to the war.

The United States has many interests in our country. The industrial, commercial, and religious enterprises under American management, have attained such proportions that we believe the Government and people of the United States ought to know the true conditions of Korea and the result of the Japanese becoming paramount in our country. We know that the people of America love fair play and advocate justice toward all men. We also know that your Excellency is the ardent exponent of a square deal between individuals as well as nations, therefore we come to you with this memorial with the hope that your Excellency may help our country at this critical period of our national life.

We fully appreciate the fact that during the conference between the Russian and Japanese peace envoys, your Excellency may not care to make any suggestion to either party as to the conditions of their settlement, but we earnestly hope that your Excellency will see to it that Korea may preserve her autonomous Government and that other Powers shall not oppress or maltreat our people. The clause in the treaty between the United States and Korea gives us a claim upon the United States for assistance, and this is the time when we need it most.

Very respectfully,
Your obedient servants,

(*Sgd.*)   P. K. Yoon.
Syngman Rhee.

J

AMERICAN POLICY IN THE CASES OF KOREA AND BELGIUM [1]

The Special Envoy of the Korean Emperor tells for the time the full story of his attempt to get President Roosevelt to intervene against Japan.

By Homer B. Hulbert

A few weeks ago I published in *The Times* a letter asserting that Theodore Roosevelt's attack upon President Wilson for his failure to protest against Germany's attack upon Belgium came with poor grace from a man who himself was guilty of a far more reprehensible breach of international obligation in 1905, when Japan forced her protectorate upon Korea.

Mr. Roosevelt has now come out with a statement that he was wholly justified in acquiescing in the extinction of Korean independence, and

[1] From the *New York Times*, March 5, 1916.

he makes the specific charges that my statement was consciously false when I said that he was aware, in advance, of the contents of the letter which I brought to him from the Emperor of Korea. In view of this charge there is nothing left me to do but to give a full and detailed account of the entire transaction and leave it to the American people to judge whether Korea received a fair deal at the hands of the Roosevelt Administration.

At the beginning of the Japanese-Russian War the Korean Government declared its neutrality, but the Japanese ignored this declaration and committed a direct breach of international law in landing troops on the soil of the peninsula. The fact that the Korean army was too small to oppose this act detracts nothing from the culpability of Japan. Having entered the country thus illegally, Japan hastened to make a treaty with Korea whereby the latter virtually became her ally in the war and put herself in jeopardy of lawful seizure and annexation by Russia in case of Russia's ultimate success. In this treaty Japan specifically guaranteed the sovereignty of Korea from molestation. It was a war measure necessitated by the circumstances and was of a temporary character merely. In allowing Japan to take charge of the communications of the empire, Korea merely acted up to the spirit of the alliance, which was that Japan should be given every facility to prosecute the war against Russia. Whether this was pleasing to the

Korean Government or not has nothing whatever to do with the legal aspect of the case.
None of the treaty powers took any action that
indicated in any way their impression that this
treaty was a genuine impairment of Korean
autonomy, as indeed it could not be if its terms
were faithfully lived up to. For Theodore
Roosevelt to say that Japan by this act virtually
assumed a protectorate over Korea shows either
that he has only the most rudimentary notions
of international law or else that the wish was
father to the thought. It was no more an impairment of Korea's sovereignty than the presence of British troops in France is an impairment of French sovereignty.

But after the war was over it soon became apparent that Japan had no intention of carrying
out her treaty obligations. The Emperor of
Korea became convinced that the autonomy of
his country was about to be impaired by his
ally, the Emperor of Japan. This being the
case, the time had arrived when the first clause
in the treaty between Korea and the United
States might rightly be cited. The Emperor
asked me to be the bearer of a message to
President Roosevelt, calling upon him to imple-
ment that clause of the treaty.

Now, I had been favourable to the Japanese
side in the struggle against Russia, as is amply
proved by my editorials in the *Korea Review*, of
which I was the editor and proprietor. I realized that the military weakness of Korea would
give Japan a chance to say that a protectorate

over the country would be necessary for Japan's safety. I therefore advised the Emperor that his appeal would be greatly strengthened if he should insert the statement that if it seemed proper to the United States and the other treaty powers interested, Korea would consent to the establishment of a joint protectorate over Korea for a period of years until things should have been so adjusted that the permanent neutrality of the country would be assured. The Emperor inserted such a clause in the letter. Having received this document for transmission, I immediately went to the United States Minister in Seoul, Mr. E. V. Morgan, and made a clear and full statement of my mission. I told him I was about to start for America with a letter to President Roosevelt from the Emperor, asking the American Government to interfere with its good offices to prevent the unlawful seizure of Korea by Japan, which seemed to be threatening. I did not propose to indulge in any clandestine operations which might embarrass my own Government. Naturally I did not make any public statement of my intentions, although several of my friends in Seoul were aware of the purpose of my going.

Mr. Morgan listened with interest to what I had to say, made no objection of any kind, and even went so far as to advise me that when I arrived in America I should retain a good international lawyer to help me put the matter through. Not only so, but he allowed me to send the document to America in the legation mail pouch, for I was somewhat in fear that the Japanese might take it from my person as I passed through Japan on my way.

There was considerable gossip in Seoul over my sudden resignation from the service of the Korean Government and my departure from Korea with my family so promptly, and the Japanese doubtless divined the cause back of it. On the day before I started the Japanese Chargé d'Affaires in Seoul met me and urged me not to go, giving various plausible reasons, and finally making some broad hints at substantial financial advantages that I should enjoy by giving up my contemplated trip.   However, I went.

I sailed from Yokohama on the *China*, of the Pacific Mail Steamship Line.   Just before we sailed a spy in the employ of the Japanese came aboard.   I recognized him, and just for the fun of the thing I kept out of his way till just a moment before the anchor was raised.   Then I came upon him suddenly.   He started perceptibly and stammered out something about my going on the *China* or the *Empress of China*, which sailed the same hour.   I laughed and said that I was booked for the *China*.   I have always regretted that I did not change over to the *Empress* boat after he went ashore, for I should have reached Washington four days earlier. At this point I would like to ask any reasonable American citizen whether it is possible to believe that Mr. Morgan did not notify the Washington Government by cable and secure instructions in the premises.   If he did not do so it was a gross breach of diplomatic duty. It is simply unthinkable.

The Japanese authorities immediately began to bring pressure on the Emperor and his Cabinet to grant a Japanese protectorate. They were met by a firm refusal. The Emperor held firm, and declared that under no circumstances would he consent to such an impairment of Korea's suzerain rights. Again and again the Japanese returned to the attack, but without success. Meanwhile I passed Honolulu, San Francisco, Chicago, Pittsburg, and was only one day from Washington. Japan had not yet been able to force her "protection" upon Korea. But it had to be done at any cost, either of ethics or of blood.

That night, while I was crossing the Cumberland Mountains, the Japanese seized the palace in Seoul, filled it with gendarmes and police, blocked every approach to the Emperor, brought the Emperor and his Cabinet together, and peremptorily demanded that they sign the death warrant of Korean independence. The Emperor and all his Ministers refused pointblank. Entreaties, flatteries, threats, all were unavailing. But the reader may say, " How do you know? You were in America." This is how I know. In 1909, in the City of Seoul, at two o'clock in the morning, escaping from the espionage of fifteen or more Japanese spies, I climbed over the back wall of my compound, made my way down through the tortuous streets of that city until I reached the home of

Han Kyu-Sul, who was Prime Minister at the time the deed was performed. I spent the rest of the night with him, and it is from his lips I heard the damning details. All the older residents of Seoul knew Han Kyu-Sul as a thorough gentleman, against whom, even in that Oriental country, there had never been a suspicion of graft or official indirection. I would take his word as implicitly as my own brother's. And this is what happened:

The Japanese, made desperate by the failure of cajolery and menace, took Han Kyu-Sul, the Premier, into a side room. There Field Marshal Hasegawa and Minister Hayashi demanded his consent. He refused. Hasegawa drew his sword on the unarmed man, but he stood firm. They left him there under guard and went back to the rest of the Cabinet. These men believed that Han Kyu-Sul had been killed, and they were, from their standpoint, justified in their suspicions. I should have believed the same thing. Three of them capitulated and signed the document. The Emperor never signed it, nor did his Prime Minister, nor were these three traitors given orders by the Emperor to sign. It is said, with what truth I cannot say, that the Japanese themselves stole the Great Seal of State from the Foreign Office and themselves affixed it to the paper. This seal was affixed within sixty minutes of my arrival at the railway station in Washington, D. C.

I immediately secured the Emperor's letter from the friend in Washington, to whom it had been sent, as I have said, in the legation mail pouch. I then consulted an old-time acquaintance of mine, who held, and still holds, a high official position at Washington, and asked him the best way to approach the President, since I was unacquainted with the rules of etiquette which govern such transactions. This friend sent a message to the President telling him that I had arrived in Washington from the Emperor of Korea with an important communication. The answer came back that, since it was a diplomatic matter, the President could not see me himself, but that the missive should be taken to the State Department.

I hastened to do so, but was told that the Secretary of State was extremely busy and that I had better come the following day. They were too busy to receive a message from a friendly power that was in its death throes! I went straight to the President's office building adjoining the White House and asked to see the President's secretary. This was refused me, but I was met by an under-secretary, whose name I never ascertained, who very blandly said, " Mr. Hulbert, we know all about this letter. You have been given instructions to go to the State Department. Nothing can be done here."

There seemed to be nothing for it but to wait. Meanwhile I was being importuned by the newspaper men to divulge the purpose of my coming. Why should they have pressed the matter so strongly? I had told no one of my mission excepting those who would be discreet.

I see here another evidence that the fact had leaked out through official channels. Therefore, the men at the head of affairs must have known the nature of my mission. It is one of the keenest regrets of my life that I did not, then and there, make a full statement for the press, and tell the American people that the Emperor of a friendly power was standing at the door of this Government demanding without avail a courteous hearing. But I thought it would be discourteous to the President and to the Secretary of State to divulge the matter before I had laid it before them.   Discourteous!

The following day I went to the State Department and asked admittance to the Secretary of State. I was told that this was the day when the various Ambassadors and Ministers from other countries were accustomed to call on the Secretary and that for this reason it would be impossible to see him. I had better come next day! On that day the American Government accepted Japan's unsupported statement that the protectorate had been secured and that it was all satisfactory to the Korean Government. Without a word of inquiry at the Korean Legation at Washington, without a word to the Emperor of Korea, without a single diplomatic formality in consideration of the Korean people and Government, the American Administration accepted Japan's bald statement, cabled the American Minister in Seoul to close the legation and broke off friendly intercourse with a treaty power, weak, to be sure, and needing all things, but a power to which we had been saying for twenty-five years that America stands for a square deal, for right as against mere brute force, a power that had given to Americans more opportunities for productive enterprise than to all other peoples combined, a power to which we had given our promise that if in her hour of need she should appeal to us we would exert our good offices in her behalf.

The next day I was allowed to see the Secretary of State. Assistant Secretaries Bacon and Adee were present, and perhaps one or two others. I do not remember.

Now I had made what may be called a technical mistake. I had consented to act as a messenger from the Emperor without receiving from him any credentials except the message which I brought. I came simply to transmit the document and let that speak for itself. Nor did this Government, either then or later, question the genuineness of that missive, as indeed, they could not well have done since it bore the Emperor's private seal.

The Secretary of State asked Assistant Secretary Adee whether, in view of the fact that I bore no special credentials, the matter could be discussed with me. The reply was that it could not. The Secretary of State received the document, then turned to me in a very pointed manner, which may not have been but certainly sounded like a rebuke: " Mr. Hulbert, do you want us to get into trouble with Japan? "

Coming upon the expert decision of Assistant

Secretary Adee that I was in no position to discuss the matter, this question nettled me a trifle and I declined to discuss it. I have sometimes wished that I had not, and yet perhaps it was as well, for if I had said anything it would have been this: " If it lies between the stultification of the American Government and trouble I will take the trouble every time," but of course this might have been considered discourteous! I said that I was merely commissioned to deliver the document, and then retired.

I am told that a few days after this occurred one of the most eminent international lawyers in America went to Secretary Root with a copy of the Korean treaty, placed his finger on that first clause in which we guarantee to use our good offices for Korea, and asked the Secretary to read it; and that when the Secretary had read it he exclaimed, " I did not know that was there."

The following day I received a cablegram from the Emperor. It had been taken over to Chefoo by boat so as to escape transmission by Japanese lines. In it the Emperor declared that the treaty was null and void, that it had been secured at the point of the sword, that it had been wrested from his Foreign Minister under duress, and that he himself had never signed it or acquiesced in its signature.

I took that cablegram to the State Department. I was received by Assistant Secretary Bacon, who took the cablegram and said that it would be put on file, or words to that effect. A few days later I received from Secretary Root a letter referring to the document that I had placed in his hands, and saying that since the Emperor of Korea had desired secrecy to be observed and had already taken final action in this matter referred to, it would be impossible for the American Government to move in the matter.

No, our Government had done all its moving earlier in the game. Why the matter of secrecy should have been brought up I do not know. The Emperor is no such novice in politics as to suppose that the American Government could have moved to help Korea without letting the Japanese Government suspect that he (the Emperor) had appealed for such help. They did not expect me to shout the matter from the housetops, I should fancy.

Soon after this I returned to Korea. I was told there by some friends that Mr. Morgan had, perhaps inadvertently, intimated that " We knew that Japan was going to take Korea, but we did not expect it quite so soon."

This brings up the question why it was that two months before the seizure of Korea by Japan the American Minister at Seoul, Dr. H. N. Allen, was suddenly recalled and Mr. E. V. Morgan put in his place. I believe an effort was made to learn the reason, that the President and the Secretary of State were non-committal, but that another member of the Cabinet intimated that Dr. H. N. Allen was so friendly with the royal family in Seoul that without a change in the legation it would be difficult for the Administration to carry out the policy upon which it had determined.

One question remains. When was that policy determined upon? I do not know; but taking all things into consideration, and putting two and two together, I am forced to believe that it was determined upon at the time of the Portsmouth Treaty.

This is a correct account, so far as I can remember, of the seizure of Korea by Japan and the part that our Government played in it. Some of my statements can be corroborated by others, some rest upon my unsupported word, but the part that can be corroborated is sufficient to prove my main contention.

I am quite willing to grant that my belief in President Roosevelt's previous knowledge of the contents of that letter rests upon circumstantial evidence, but I ask the American people to decide for themselves whether his memory is not, perhaps, slightly at fault when he declares that he did not know the exact wording but the essential gist and purport of the letter several days before it was delivered. I trust it is within the bounds of courtesy to ask him to tell the people of this country why the message from the Emperor was held off for two days until he had taken action in the matter. If he was at that time convinced that Korea's autonomy was already injured beyond repair, why did he not receive the message and answer it according to the tenor of his belief? If he says that it was because I had no credentials, how comes it that he did not also know what I had come to do without credentials? I ask him how it came about that one of his under-secretaries in the White House knew more about the contents of that letter than he himself did.

In conclusion, I may say that in my estimation comparatively little blame should rest upon Elihu Root in this matter. He was necessarily under instructions. Whether those instructions were agreeable to him or not the world will never know, but I hope they were not. To my mind he was less culpable than unfortunate.

K

KOREA UNDER JAPAN [1]

Henry Chung

" If the lips are destroyed, the teeth get cold." This is a literal translation of a Korean proverb, Chinese in origin. The Chinese orator and diplomat in the feudal period of the Chow dynasty who originated this epigram conceived, long before the birth of European nations, the principle of balance of power as necessary to the peace and independence of nations contiguous in territory. At the opening of the twentieth century Korea was the lips and China was the teeth. Now the lips are destroyed, and the unprotected surface of the Chinese teeth are ex-

[1] From the *Chinese Students' Monthly*, vol. XIII, No. 7, pp. 400-403, May, 1918.

posed to the corrosion of Japanese aggression. Every Chinese who carries the welfare of his Fatherland in his heart ought, therefore, to study with vital interest the recent history of Korea, for there we find the example of what may befall China, unless the present tendency of Japanese imperial expansion on Asiatic mainland is checkmated either by China herself or by a concerted action of Western powers in the Eastern theatre of international politics.

In destroying a nation—if the destruction be complete—two things are essential: economic subjection and spiritual massacre. The former is a comparatively easy matter as its execution is based entirely on physical force, but the latter requires time and assiduous effort on the part of the conquering nation. Japan, profiting by the experience of the colonizing nations of the West, is applying in Korea a method the most unique and effective known in the history of imperial conquests. When Bismarck wanted to Prussianize Poland, he moved several million Germans into German Poland to help assimilate the Poles. Money was appropriated by the German Government to buy land from the Poles for these newcomers. The Poles clung to their lands and refused to be assimilated, with the consequence that the price of land in German Poland went up and the Poles became prosperous. Japan pursued the same policy in a more efficacious way. The Oriental Colonization Company was organized under the direction of the government, and is supported by an annual subsidy of 500,000 yen ($250,000) from the imperial treasury. Its purpose is to colonize Korea with Japanese who are unable to make a living in Japan proper. A Japanese emigrant is given free transportation to Korea, and is provided with a home and a piece of land together with necessary implements and provisions when he gets there. He is expected to pay back to the company in three or four years what he thus receives. For this purpose the Japanese Government in Korea confiscated all public lands formerly under the control of local communities, and all lands owned by Buddhist temples and cultivated by Buddhist priests. But these were far from being enough to meet the demand. Korea has an area of 80,000 square miles inhabited by 15,000,000 agricultural population. The Oriental Colonization Company tried to buy lands from the Koreans, but the Koreans refused to sell them. Here the government aid was brought in. All financial machinery in Korea is controlled by the Bank of Chosen, a government bank in Seoul. This powerful financial institution through its branch banks and agencies called in all the specie in the country and made the land practically moneyless as far as the circulating medium was concerned. Cash the Koreans must have to pay taxes and to buy the necessities of life. The only way they could get money was to sell their real estate. The value of land dropped to one-half, in many localities as low as one-fifth, of its original value. Then the Bank of Chosen sent out agents all over the country and bought the land for tens of thousands of Japanese emigrants sent over by the Oriental Colonization Company. This process has been repeated time and again. The Koreans know the game of the government, but they have no means to counteract this government speculation. Technically, the Japanese Government in Korea has never carried on a wholesale confiscation of individual property, but this governmental speculation is nothing short of confiscation. Already more than one-fifth of the richest land in Korea is in the hands of the Japanese, and the amount is increasing steadily.

In commerce and industry, the Japanese have the complete monopoly. While Korea was independent, all nations enjoyed equal commercial privileges. Now the Nipponese tradesmen practically drive out all other nationals and have the market to themselves. The Korean merchant cannot compete with his Japanese competitor because of the preferential treatment shown by the government. All the rights to develop the resources of the country are given to the Japanese, and Korean enterprise, even of the humblest sort, is insidiously hampered by the Japanese. Thus the Korean people are reduced to industrial serfdom, and are forced to submit to Japanese rule through economic pressure.

The Korean has a proud history and a civilization of four thousand years back of him, and he is unwilling to abandon his traditional culture under any circumstances. Something more than mere economic pressure and political domination is needed to extinguish the soul of Korea. History and literature are the records of past achievements, and language is the medium of expression that gives birth to the pregnant genius. The Japanese statesmen fully appreciate the importance of this triple support of national consciousness. They made a systematic collection of all works of Korean history and literature in public archives and private homes and burned them. This is undoubtedly the greatest injustice that the Korean people have suffered at the hands of the Japanese. Korean scholars consider this as an irreparable loss second only to the destruction of the Alexandrian Library by Omar in 640. Priceless treasures have been destroyed in this needless vandalism of the Japanese. All Korean periodical literature—from local newspapers to scientific journals—has been completely stamped out. In order to create in the West a favourable impression of their rule in Korea, the Japanese Government has a subsidized organ, the *Seoul Press*. This daily, published in English, disseminates only the kind of news that the Japanese wish to have known in the West. It is an official camouflage. This publicity channel is further strengthened by the " Annual Report on Reforms and Progress in Chosen," a well illustrated volume published in English by the government, and sent out gratis to all great men and large libraries in America and Great Britain. These publications picture vividly the " contentment and prosperity " that the Japanese rule is bringing to the Koreans. And what they say usually find echoes in the West through a few men who have been decorated in Japan with gold war medals and the insignias of the Rising Sun. These men take delight in returning the favours that they have received in Japan by singing the glory and grandeur of Japanese Asiatic policy, and by picturing Japanese administration in Korea as a " benevolent assimilation." [2]

The Japanese language has been made the official tongue, not only in official documents but in schools and public gatherings. Here the Christian Church stands as an obstacle. A vast majority of Korean Christians cannot read Japanese, and the church services cannot be intelligibly conducted in a foreign tongue. To curb the spreading influence of Christianity and to crush out completely the one obstacle to the denationalizing of Korea, the Governor General Terauchi (now Premier of Japan), in 1912, instituted what is known in the church annals of Korea as " The Persecution of the Church." Prominent church men, leaders in Korean thought and education, were charged with conspiracy and put in prison, and their activities ended. Prominent American missionaries were brought in the trial as being connected with the conspiracy to assassinate the governor general of Korea. Here, however, the Japanese over-

---

[2] See G. T. Ladd, "Annexation of Korea: An Essay in Benevolent Assimilation," *Yale Review* n. s. 1 : 639-656, July, 1912.

stepped themselves. Their charges against the Korean church aroused considerable criticism in the West, and when they saw that their attempt was producing a reaction, they stopped the persecution of the Korean Christians, and satisfied themselves in limiting the activities of the church. At present there is pending a negotiation between the Japanese authorities and the missionary body in Korea concerning the missionary schools in the peninsula. The mission schools in Korea have been deprived of their former rights under the old Korean administration, and are denied the privileges that Christian mission schools enjoy in Japan proper. They are insidiously discriminated against by the Japanese authorities on the ground that they serve as the hiding places of Korean nationalism.[*]

Under pretext of unifying the educational system of Korea and bringing it up to a "higher standard," the Japanese Government in Korea passed educational regulations which forbid religious services and the teaching of history, geography, and the Korean language in all the schools in Korea. Furthermore, they provide that all Korean schools shall be under the strict supervision of Japanese educators, and that the Korean children shall be taught to salute the Japanese flag and worship the Japanese Emperor's tablet. Korean students who go to

[*] A full discussion of the negotiation between the Japanese authorities and the missionaries in Korea concerning the school regulations is given by Arthur Judson Brown in *International Review of Missions*, VI: 74–99, January, 1917.

Japan to complete their education are advised to attend trade or technical schools, but they are practically barred from higher institutions of learning. It is almost impossible for a Korean student to specialize in such subjects as law, history or economics in the Imperial University at Tokyo, and no Korean student is permitted to go to Europe or America to finish his education. "Korea has been Prussianized," says Tyler Dennett, who has visited the East twice, once as a magazine writer, and later in connection with the Centenary Commission of the Methodist Episcopal Church. "Japan has even gone so far as to forbid Korean students to come to the United States to finish their education. The Prussianizing of Alsace-Lorraine never went to such an extent as that."[4]

The tragedy in the case of the Korean is that he suffers the fate of a conquered race, alike with the Poles and the Bohemians, yet his plight is unknown to the outside world. Japan knows the value of honourable intentions in the public opinion of the West, so she, through the clever manipulation of publicity propaganda, has created an impression in the West that she is a gallant knight that guards Asia from the European dragon. She compares her position toward Korea and China with that of the United States toward the Philippines and Mexico, and has announced, through the Lansing-Ishii agreement of last year, her imperial policy in the

[4] Tyler Dennett, "The Road to Peace, via China," *Outlook,* 117: 168–169, October 3, 1917.

East as the "Asiatic Monroe Doctrine." The same policy that undermined Korea—the policy of an opportunist with all its necessary accompaniment of deceit, cajolery, intimidation, and treachery—is in full operation in China. In the same manner as she professed to guarantee the political independence and territorial integrity of Korea up to the very eve of the destruction of Korean independence, Japan now declares that "Japan not only will not seek to assail the integrity or the sovereignty of China, but will eventually be prepared to defend and maintain the integrity and independence of China against any aggressor," as Viscount Ishii puts it. Indeed, it would be the greatest of all tragedies in the world's history, should China, the oldest of nations and the cradle of Oriental civilization, follow the footsteps of Korea into the pit of national destruction. Will China awake to the impending danger before it is too late?

L

THE ROOT-TAKAHIRA AGREEMENT DECLARING THE MUTUAL POLICY OF THE UNITED STATES AND JAPAN IN THE FAR EAST

Imperial Japanese Embassy,
Washington, November 30, 1918.

SIR:
The exchange of views between us, which

has taken place at the several interviews which I have recently had the honour of holding with you, has shown that Japan and the United States holding important outlying insular possessions in the region of the Pacific Ocean, the Governments of the two countries are animated by a common aim, policy, and intention in that region.

Believing that a frank avowal of that aim, policy, and intention would not only tend to strengthen the relations of friendship and good neighbourhood, which have immemorially existed between Japan and the United States, but would materially contribute to the preservation of the general peace, the Imperial Government have authorized me to present to you an outline of their understanding of that common aim, policy, and intention:

1. It is the wish of the two Governments to encourage the free and peaceful development of their commerce on the Pacific Ocean.

2. The policy of both Governments, uninfluenced by any aggressive tendencies, is directed to the maintenance of the existing *status quo* in the region above mentioned and to the defense of the principle of equal opportunity for commerce and industry in China.

3. They are accordingly firmly resolved reciprocally to respect the territorial possessions belonging to each other in said region.

4. They are also determined to preserve the common interest of all powers in China by supporting by all pacific means at their disposal the

independence and integrity of China and the principle of equal opportunity for commerce and industry of all nations in that Empire.

5. Should any event occur threatening the *status quo* as above described or the principle of equal opportunity as above defined, it remains for the two Governments to communicate with each other in order to arrive at an understanding as to what measures they may consider it useful to take.

If the foregoing outline accords with the view of the Government of the United States, I shall be gratified to receive your confirmation.

I take this opportunity to renew to Your Excellency the assurance of my highest consideration.

K. TAKAHIRA.

HONORABLE ELIHU ROOT,
Secretary of State.

Department of State,
Washington, November 30, 1908.

EXCELLENCY:

I have the honour to acknowledge the receipt of your note of to-day setting forth the result of the exchange of views between us in our recent interviews defining the understanding of the two Governments in regard to their policy in the region of the Pacific Ocean.

It is a pleasure to inform you that this expression of mutual understanding is welcome to the Government of the United States as appropriate to the happy relations of the two countries and as the occasion for a concise mutual affirmation of that accordant policy respecting the Far East which the two Governments have so frequently declared in the past.

I am happy to be able to confirm to Your Excellency, on behalf of the United States, the declaration of the two Governments embodied in the following words:

1. It is the wish of the two Governments to encourage the free and peaceful development of their commerce on the Pacific Ocean.

2. The policy of both Governments, uninfluenced by any aggressive tendencies, is directed to the maintenance of the existing *status quo* in the region above mentioned, and to the defense of the principle of equal opportunity for commerce and industry in China.

3. They are accordingly firmly resolved reciprocally to respect the territorial possessions belonging to each other in said region.

4. They are also determined to preserve the common interests of all powers in China by supporting by all pacific means at their disposal the independence and integrity of China and the principle of equal opportunity for commerce and industry of all nations in that Empire.

5. Should any event occur threatening the *status quo* as above described or the principle of equal opportunity as above defined, it remains for the two Governments to communicate with each other in order to arrive at an understanding as to what measures they may consider it useful to take.

Accept, Excellency, the renewed assurance of my highest consideration.

ELIHU ROOT.

His Excellency
BARON KOGORA TAKAHIRA,
Japanese Ambassador.

M

THE PREMIER OF JAPAN TO THE AMERICAN PEOPLE

A Message from Count Okuma.[1]

I gladly seize the opportunity to send, through the medium of *The Independent*, a message to the people of the United States, who have always been helpful and loyal friends of Japan.

It is my desire to convince your people of the sincerity of my Government and of my people in all their utterances and assurances connected with the present regrettable situation in Europe and the Far East.

Every sense of loyalty and honour oblige Japan to coöperate with Great Britain to clear from these waters the enemies who in the past, the present and the future menace her interests, her trade, her shipping and her people's lives.

This Far Eastern situation is not of our seeking.

[1] Published in *The Independent* (New York), August 31, 1914.

It was ever my desire to maintain peace as will be amply proved; as President of the Peace Society of Japan I have consistently so endeavoured.

I have read with admiration the lofty message of President Wilson to his people on the subject of neutrality.

We, of Japan, are appreciative of the spirit and motive that prompted the head of your great nation and we feel confident that his message will meet with a national response.

As Premier of Japan I have stated and I now again state to the people of America and of the world that Japan has no ulterior motive, no desire to secure more territory, no thought of depriving China or any other peoples of anything which they now possess.

My Government and my people have given their word and their pledge, which will be as honourably kept as Japan always keeps promises.

Tokyo, August 24, 1914.

N

THE TWENTY-ONE DEMANDS

Official translation of Document handed to President Yuan Shi Kai by Mr. Hioki, the Japanese Minister, on January 18, 1915.

GROUP I

The Japanese Government and the Chinese Government being desirous of maintaining the

peace of Eastern Asia and of further strength-
ening the friendly relations existing between
the two neighbouring nations, agree to the following Articles:

Article 1.—The Chinese Government agrees
that when the Japanese Government hereafter
approaches the German Government for the
transfer of all rights and privileges of whatsoever nature enjoyed by Germany in the Province of Shantung, whether secured by Treaty
or in any other manner, China shall give her
full assent thereto.

Article 2.—The Chinese Government agrees
that within the Province of Shantung and
along its sea border no territory or island of any
name or nature shall be ceded or leased to any
third Power.

Article 3.—The Chinese Government consents
to Japan's building a railway from Chefoo or
Lungkou to join the Kiaochow-Tsinanfu Railway.

Article 4.—The Chinese Government engages,
in the interest of trade and for the residence of
foreigners, to open by herself as soon as possible
certain important cities and towns in the Province of Shantung as commercial ports. What
places shall be opened are to be jointly decided
upon in a separate agreement.

Group II

The Japanese Government and the Chinese
Government, since the Chinese Government has
always acknowledged the special position en-

joyed by Japan in South Manchuria and Eastern Inner Mongolia, agree to the following articles:

Article 1.—The two contracting parties mutually agree that the term of lease of Port Arthur and Dalny and the term of lease of the South Manchurian Railway and the Antung-Mukden Railway shall be extended to the period of ninety-nine years.

Article 2.—Japanese subjects in South Manchuria and Eastern Inner Mongolia shall have the right to lease or own land required either for erecting suitable buildings for trade and manufacture or for farming.

Article 3.—Japanese subjects shall be free to reside and travel in South Manchuria and Eastern Inner Mongolia and to engage in business and in manufacture of any kind whatsoever.

Article 4.—The Chinese Government agrees to grant to Japanese subjects the right of opening the mines in South Manchuria and Eastern Mongolia. As regards what mines are to be opened, they shall be decided upon jointly.

Article 5.—The Chinese Government agrees that in respect of the (two) cases mentioned herein below the Japanese Government's consent shall be first obtained before action is taken:

(*a*) Whenever permission is granted to the subject of a third Power to build a railway or to make a loan with a third Power for the purpose of building a railway in South Manchuria and Eastern Inner Mongolia.

(*b*) Whenever a loan is to be made with a

third Power pledging the local taxes of South
Manchuria and Eastern Inner Mongolia as security.

Article 6.—The Chinese Government agrees
that if the Chinese Government employs political, financial or military advisers or instructors
in South Manchuria or Eastern Mongolia, the
Japanese Government shall first be consulted.

Article 7.—The Chinese Government agrees
that the control and management of the Kirin-
Changchun Railway shall be handed over to the
Japanese Government for a term of ninety-nine
years dating from the signing of this agreement.

GROUP III

The Japanese Government and the Chinese
Government, seeing that Japanese financiers
and the Hanyehping Company have close relations with each other at present and desiring
that the common interests of the two nations
shall be advanced, agree to the following articles:

Article 1.—The two contracting parties mutually agree that when the opportune moment arrives the Hanyehping Company shall be made a
joint concern of the two nations and they
further agree that without the previous consent
of Japan, China shall not by her own act dispose
of the rights and property of whatsoever nature
of the said company nor cause the said company
to dispose freely of the same.

Article 2.—The Chinese Government agrees
that all mines in the neighbourhood of those

owned by the Hanyehping Company shall not
be permitted, without the consent of the said
company, to be worked by other persons outside
of the said company; and further agrees that if
it is desired to carry out any undertaking which,
it is apprehended, may directly or indirectly affect the interests of the said company, the consent of the said company shall first be obtained.

GROUP IV

The Japanese Government and the Chinese
Government with the object of effectively preserving the territorial integrity of China agree
to the following special article:

The Chinese Government engages not to cede
or lease to a third Power any harbour or bay or
island along the coast of China.

GROUP V

Article 1.—The Chinese Central Government
shall employ influential Japanese as advisers in
political, financial, and military affairs.

Article 2.—Japanese hospitals, churches and
schools in the interior of China shall be granted
the right of owning land.

Article 3.—Inasmuch as the Japanese Government and the Chinese Government have had
many cases of dispute between Japanese and
Chinese police which caused no little misunderstanding, it is for this reason necessary that the
police departments of important places (in
China) shall be jointly administered by Japanese and Chinese or that the police departments

of these places shall employ numerous Japanese, so that they may at the same time help to plan for the improvement of the Chinese Police Service.

Article 4.—China shall purchase from Japan a fixed amount of munitions of war (say 50 per cent. or more of what is needed by the Chinese Government) or that there shall be established in China a Sino-Japanese jointly worked arsenal. Japanese technical experts are to be employed and Japanese material to be purchased.

Article 5.—China agrees to grant to Japan the right of constructing a railway connecting Wuchang with Kiukiang and Nanchang, another line between Nanchang and Hangchow, and another between Nanchang and Chaochou.

Article 6.—If China needs foreign capital to work mines, build railways and construct harbour works (including dockyards) in the Province of Fukien, Japan shall be first consulted.

Article 7.—China agrees that Japanese subjects shall have the right of missionary propaganda in China.

O

A RÉSUMÉ OF JAPAN'S PROCEDURE IN CONNECTION WITH THE TWENTY-ONE DEMANDS [1]

(*a*) Presentation of demands in *twenty-one* ar-

[1] From Millard, " Our Eastern Question," pp. 147–148.

ticles, coupled with a strong admonition to China that both haste and secrecy were insisted on by Japan.

(b) Continuous pressure on China to force her to concede the demands *en bloc*, without discussion.

(c) Repeated warning to China not to inform other Powers of the negotiations, even confidentially.

(d) First publications of news about the demands were categorically and officially denied by Japan.

(e) Newspapers in Japan were warned by the Government not to publish or discuss news about the demands.

(f) Japan's diplomatic representatives abroad were instructed to deny and discredit news about the demands.

(g) The Minister at Peking denied to inquiries of other legations that any demands had been made.

(h) When copies of the original demands, procured from the Chinese Government, were received by other foreign Governments, Japan still denied the twenty-one demands, and presented a list of eleven articles, omitting the most objectionable matters.

P

THE REVISED DEMANDS

PRESENTED BY MR. HIOKI, THE JAPANESE MINISTER,
TO THE CHINESE GOVERNMENT ON APRIL 26,
1915, YIELDED TO BY THE CHINESE GOV-
ERNMENT ON MAY 8, 1915

GROUP I

The Japanese Government and the Chinese
Government being desirous of maintaining the
peace of Eastern Asia and of further strength-
ening the friendly relations existing between
the two neighbouring nations agree to the following articles:

Article 1.—The Chinese Government agrees
that when the Japanese Government hereafter
approaches the German Government for the
transfer of all rights and privileges of whatsoever nature enjoyed by Germany in the Province of Shantung, whether secured by treaty or
in any other manner, China shall give her full
assent thereto.

Article 2.—The Chinese Government engages
that within the Province of Shantung and along
its sea border no territory or island or land of
any name or nature shall be ceded or leased to
any third Power.

Article 3.—The Chinese Government consents
that as regards the railway to be built by China
herself from Chefoo or Lungkow, to connect
with the Kiaochow-Tsinanfu Railway, if Ger-

many is willing to abandon the privilege of financing the Chefoo-Weihsien line, China will approach Japanese capitalists to negotiate for a loan.

Article 4.—The Chinese Government engages, in the interest of trade and for the residence of foreigners, to open by China herself as soon as possible certain suitable places in the Province of Shantung as commercial ports.

THE FOLLOWING TO BE SUBJECT OF AN EXCHANGE OF NOTES:

The places which ought to be opened are to be chosen, and the regulations are to be drafted, by the Chinese Government, but the Japanese minister must be consulted before making a decision.

GROUP II

The Japanese Government and the Chinese Government, with a view to developing their economic relations in South Manchuria and Eastern Inner Mongolia, agree to the following articles:

Article 1.—The two contracting Powers mutually agree that the term of lease of Port Arthur and Dalny and the term of the South Manchurian Railway and the Antung-Mukden Railway, shall be extended to ninety-nine years.

Article 2.—Japanese subjects in South Manchuria may lease or purchase necessary land for erecting suitable buildings for trade and manufacture or for prosecuting agricultural enterprises.

Article 3.—Japanese subjects shall be free to reside and travel in South Manchuria and to engage in business and in manufacture of any kind whatsoever.

Article 3a.—The Japanese subjects referred to in the preceding two articles besides being required to register with local authorities passports, which they must procure under the existing regulations, shall also observe police laws and ordinances and tax regulations which are approved by the Japanese Consul. Civil and criminal cases in which the defendants are Japanese shall be tried and adjudicated by the Japanese Consul; those in which the defendants are Chinese shall be tried and adjudicated by Chinese authorities. In either instance the authorities on the plaintiff side can send a delegate to attend the proceedings; but mixed civil cases between Chinese and Japanese relating to land shall be tried and adjudicated by the delegates of both nations conjointly in accordance with Chinese laws and local usage. When the judicial system in the said region is completely reformed all the civil and criminal cases concerning Japanese subjects shall be tried entirely by Chinese law courts.

Article 4.—The Chinese Government agrees that Japanese subjects shall be permitted forthwith to investigate, select, and then prospect for and open mines at the following places in South Manchuria, apart from those mining areas in which mines are being prospected for or worked; until the mining ordinance is definitely settled, methods at present in force shall be followed:

PROVINCE OF FENG-TIEN

Locality	District	Mineral
Niu Hsin T'ai	Pen-hsi	Coal
Tien Shih Fu Kou	Pen-hsi	do.
Sha Sung Kang	Hai-lung	do.
T'ieh Ch'ang	T'ung-hua	do.
Nuan Ti T'ang	Chin	do.
An Shan Chan region	From Liao-yang to Pen-hsi	Iron

PROVINCE OF KIRIN (*Southern Portion*)

Sha Sung Kang	Ho-Lung	C. & I.
Kang Yao	Chi-lin (Kirin)	Coal
Chia P'i Kou	Hua-tien	Gold

Article 5.—The Chinese Government declares that China will hereafter provide funds for building railways in South Manchuria; if foreign capital is required the Chinese Government agrees to negotiate for a loan with Japanese capitalists first.

Article 5a.—The Chinese Government agrees that hereafter, when a foreign loan is to be made on the security of the taxes of South Manchuria (not including customs and salt revenue on the security of which loans have already been made by the Central Government), it will negotiate for the loan with Japanese capitalists first.

Article 6.—The Chinese Government declares that hereafter, if foreign advisers or instructors on political, financial, military, or police matters are to be employed in South Manchuria, Japanese will be employed first.

Article 7.—The Chinese Government agrees speedily to make a fundamental revision of the Kirin-Changchun Railway Loan Agreement, taking as a standard the provisions in railway loan agreements made heretofore between China and foreign financiers. If, in future, more advantageous terms than those in existing railway loan agreements are granted to foreign financiers, in connection with railway loans, the above agreement shall again be revised in accordance with Japan's wishes.

Matters Relating to Eastern Inner Mongolia

1. The Chinese Government agrees that whenever a loan is to be made with a third Power, pledging the local taxes of Eastern Inner Mongolia as security, China must negotiate with the Japanese Government first.

2. The Chinese Government agrees that China will herself provide funds for building the railways in Eastern Inner Mongolia; if foreign capital is required she must negotiate with the Japanese Government first.

3. The Chinese Government agrees, in the interest of trade and the residence of foreigners, to open by herself as soon as possible certain suitable places in Eastern Inner Mongolia as commercial ports. The places which ought to be opened are to be chosen and the regulations to be drafted by the Chinese Government, but

the Japanese Minister must be consulted before reaching a decision.

4. If there are Japanese and Chinese who desire to coöperate in agricultural enterprises, including incidental manufacture, the Chinese Government shall forthwith give its permission.

GROUP III

The relations between Japan and the Hanyehping Company being very intimate, if the said Company comes to an agreement with the Japanese capitalists for coöperation the Chinese Government shall forthwith give its consent thereto. The Chinese Government further agrees that without the consent of the Japanese capitalists China will not convert the company into a state enterprise, nor confiscate it nor cause it to borrow and use foreign capital other than Japanese.

GROUP IV

China to make a declaration by herself in accordance with the following principle: No part of China's coast, bays, harbours or islands shall be ceded or leased to another power.

GROUP V

Yangtze Railways—to be confirmed by exchange of notes

A

As regards the right of financing by loan the Wuchang-Kiukiang-Nanchang Railways, the Nanchang-Hangchow Railway, and the Nanchang-Chaochow Railway, if it is clearly ascertained that other powers have no objection China shall grant the said right to Japan.

B

As regards the right of financing by loan the Wuchang-Kiukiang-Nanchang Railways, the Nanchang-Hangchow Railway, and the Nanchang-Chaochow Railway, the Chinese Government shall promise not to *grant* the said right to *any foreign* power before Japan comes to an understanding with the power which is heretofore *interested* therein.

Fukien—to be confirmed by exchange of notes

The Chinese Government agrees that no power shall be permitted to establish along the coast of Fu-kien a dockyard, a coaling station for military use, or a naval base; nor will any other installations for military purposes be permitted. The Chinese Government further agrees that China will not use foreign capital to put up by herself the above-mentioned establishments or installations.

Mr. Lu, the Chinese Minister of Foreign Affairs, stated as follows:

1. The Chinese Government shall, whenever in future it considers this step necessary, engage numerous Japanese advisers.

2. Whenever in future Japanese subjects desire to lease or purchase land in the interior of China for establishing schools or hospitals the

Chinese Government shall forthwith give its consent thereto.

3.   When a suitable opportunity arises in the future the Chinese Government will send military officers to Japan to negotiate with Japanese military authorities the matter of purchasing arms or that of establishing joint arsenals.

Mr. Hioki, the Japanese Minister, stated as follows:

As relates to the question of propagating religion (Buddhism), the same shall be taken up again for negotiation in the future.

Q

CHINA'S REPLY TO THE JAPANESE ULTIMATUM

The reply of the Chinese Government to the Ultimatum of the Japanese Government, delivered to the Japanese Minister of Foreign Affairs on the 8th of May, 1915.

On the 7th of this month, at three o'clock P. M., the Chinese Government received an Ultimatum from the Japanese Government together with an Explanatory Note of seven articles.   The Ultimatum concluded with the hope that the Chinese Government up to six o'clock P. M. on the 9th of May, will give a satisfactory reply, and it is hereby declared that if no satisfactory reply is received before or at the designated time, the Japanese Government will take steps she may deem necessary.

The Chinese Government with a view to preserving the peace of the Far East, hereby accepts, with the exception of those five articles of Group V postponed for later negotiation, all the articles of Groups I, II, III and IV, and the exchange of notes in connection with Fukien Province in Group V as contained in the revised proposals presented on the 26th of April and in accordance with the Explanatory Note of seven articles accompanying the Ultimatum of the Japanese Government with the hope that thereby all outstanding questions are settled, so that the cordial relationship between the two countries may be further consolidated. The Japanese Minister is hereby requested to appoint a day to call at the Ministry of Foreign Affairs to make the literary improvement of the text and sign the Agreement as soon as possible.

R

AMERICAN NOTE OF PROTEST IN REGARD TO THE AGREEMENT BETWEEN JAPAN AND CHINA

Delivered to the Chinese Government by the American Minister at Peking on May 16, 1915 [1]

In view of the circumstances of the negotiations which have taken place or which are now

[1] An identical note was handed to the Japanese Government through the American embassy at Tokyo.

pending between the Government of China and the Government of Japan and the agreements which have been reached and as a result thereof, the Government of the United States has the honour to notify the Government of the Chinese Republic that it cannot recognize any agreement or undertaking which has been entered into, or which may be entered into between the Governments of China and Japan impairing the treaty rights of the United States and its citizens in China, the political or territorial integrity of the Republic of China, or the international policy, commonly known as the open door policy.

S

THE PEKING PETITION

To the President of the United States, Washington:

We whose names are subscribed to this petition and to the accompanying Memorial do most urgently beg that the American Government, in compliance with the high mandates of the Christian civilization of the twentieth century, and in defense of the vital interests of the American as well as of the Chinese republic, and in furtherance of the sacred cause of world peace on the Pacific . . . will immediately, in conjunction if possible with Great Britain and the other powers, but if necessary alone, demand of the Chinese—not the Japanese—government representation, as parties in interest, in the conferences on the Twenty-one Demands now proceeding, which demands vitally affect American and world interests guaranteed under the Open Door Agreement. We further beg that, pending the arrival of such representatives of America and of Great Britain and other powers, the Chinese and Japanese Governments shall be requested to suspend negotiations, in order that the interests of all nations may be effectively secured against infringement. And still further we beg that the governments both of China and Japan may be notified that the presence of unusual bodies of Japanese troops on Chinese soil at this time not only embarrasses freedom of negotiations but constitutes an outrage on the rights, and a serious menace to the peace and safety, of Americans and of foreigners generally, and that pending the removal of such excessive contingents of Japanese troops all negotiations should be suspended. With all sentiments of profound respect we submit this Petition and accompanying Memorial, claiming no superior wisdom but only superior opportunities of acquaintance with the situation in its present serious aspect, and in its inevitable future consequences. We request that if not incompatible with the public interest this Petition and Memorial, with our names attached, may be communicated to the Associated

Press for such further use as may serve the interests involved.

Peking, Easter, 1915.

CHARLES F. HUBBARD,
  Minister of the Union Foreign Church.
W. A. P. MARTIN,
  Ex-President of the Imperial University.
CHAUNCEY GOODRICH,
  Chairman of the Mandarin Revision Committee.
H. H. LOWRY,
  President of Peking University.
JOHN WHORRY,
  Chairman of the Union Wen-Li Bible Revision Committee.
COURTNEY H. FENN,
  Principal Union Theological College.
EDWARD W. THWING,
  Superintendent International Reform Bureau.

T

THE LANSING-ISHII AGREEMENT

Department of State,
Washington, November 2, 1917.

EXCELLENCY:

I have the honour to communicate herein my understanding of the agreement reached by us in our recent conversation touching the questions of mutual interest to our governments relating to the Republic of China.

In order to silence mischievous reports that have from time to time been circulated, it is believed by us that a public announcement once more of the desires and intentions shared by our two governments with regard to China is advisable.

The Governments of the United States and Japan recognize that territorial propinquity creates special relations between countries, and, consequently, the Government of the United States recognizes that Japan has special interests in China, particularly in the part to which her possessions are contiguous.

The territorial sovereignty of China, nevertheless, remains unimpaired, and the Government of the United States has every confidence in the repeated assurances of the Imperial Japanese Government that, while geographical position gives Japan such special interests, they have no desire to discriminate against the trade of other nations or to disregard the commercial rights heretofore granted by China in treaties with other powers.

The Governments of the United States and Japan deny that they have any purpose to infringe in any way the independence or territorial integrity of China, and they declare, furthermore, that they always adhere to the principle of the so-called "open door," or equal opportunity for commerce and industry in China.

Moreover, they mutually declare that they are opposed to the acquisition by any Government of any special rights or privileges that would affect the independence or territorial integrity of China, or that would deny to the subjects or citizens of any country the full enjoyment of equal opportunity in the commerce and industry of China.

I shall be glad to have your Excellency confirm this understanding of the agreement reached by us.

Accept, Excellency, the renewed assurance of my highest consideration.

(Signed)   ROBERT LANSING.

His Excellency, VISCOUNT KIKUJIRO ISHII,
   Ambassador Extraordinary and Plenipotentiary of Japan, on special mission.

The Special Mission of Japan,
Washington, November 2, 1917.

SIR:

I have the honour to acknowledge the receipt of your note of to-day, communicating to me your understanding of the agreement reached by us in our recent conversations touching the questions of mutual interest to our governments relating to the Republic of China.

I am happy to be able to confirm to you, under authorization of my government, the understanding in question set forth in the following terms:

[Here the Special Ambassador repeats the language of the agreement as given in Secretary Lansing's note.]

(Signed)   K. ISHII.

Ambassador Extraordinary and Plenipotentiary of Japan, on special mission.

Honorable ROBERT LANSING,
   Secretary of State.

U

THE NEW SINO-JAPANESE MILITARY AGREEMENT

The Substance of the Secret Agreement Concluded on March 19, 1918, between Premier Tuan Chi-jui of China and the Japanese Military Commission in Peking.[1] (From *Millard's Review*, Shanghai, China, May 25, 1918.)

Just why there has been so much secrecy concerning the nature of the negotiations between Japan and China which are now said to be terminated if indeed they are of so excellent a nature as the guarded statements concerning them would lead one to believe, is rather hard to understand. . . . The public can gain some sort of an idea as to the nature of the new agreement by a perusal of the following translation of the purported agreement as it has been made public in some of the native newspapers:

Article I.—In view of the penetration of enemy influence into the eastern territory of Russia, and of the likelihood of the peace of the two contracting parties being disturbed thereby, China and Japan mutually agree actively to undertake the obligations of war participation by measures designed jointly to guard against the action of the enemy.

[1] A full discussion of the agreement is given in *Millard's Review* (Shanghai), May 25, 1918, vol. IV, pp. 453–455, 457–463, 480–483.

Article II.—The two countries shall mutually recognize and respect the equality of the other regarding position and interests in carrying out joint military measures.

Article III.—When it is necessary to take action based on this agreement, orders will be issued by both China and Japan to their troops and people, calling on them to be frankly sincere in dealing with each other in the area of military operations; and the Chinese officials shall coöperate and assist the Japanese troops in the area involved so that there may be no hindrance to military movements. Japanese troops shall on their part respect Chinese sovereignty and shall not cause any inconvenience to the Chinese people by violating local customs and traditions.

Article IV.—Japanese troops in Chinese territory shall withdraw from China as soon as war is ended.

Article V.—If it be found necessary to send troops outside of Chinese territory, troops will be jointly sent by the two countries.

Article VI.—The war area and war responsibilities shall be fixed by mutual arrangement of the military authorities of the two countries as and when occasion arises in accordance with their respective military resources.

Article VII.—In the interests of convenience, the military authorities of the two countries shall undertake the following affairs during the period necessary for the execution of joint measures:—

1. The two countries shall mutually assist

and facilitate each other in extending the means of communications (post and telegraph) in connection with military movements and transportation.

2. When necessary for war purposes construction operations may be carried on and the same shall be decided, when occasion arises, by mutual consent of the chief commanders of the two countries. The said construction-operations shall be removed when the war is ended.

3. The two countries shall mutually supply each other with military supplies and raw materials for the purpose of jointly guarding against the enemy. The quantity to be supplied shall be limited to the extent of not interfering with the necessary requirements of the country supplying the same.

4. Regarding questions of military sanitation in the war area the two countries shall render mutual assistance to each other.

5. Officers directly concerned with war operations shall mutually be sent by the two countries for coöperation (the two countries shall exchange staff officers for military coöperations?). If one party should ask for the assistance of technical experts, the other shall supply the same.

6. For convenience; military maps of the area of war operations will be exchanged.

Article VIII.—When the Chinese Eastern Railway is used for military transportation, the provisions of the original treaty relating to the management and protection of the said line shall be respected. The method of transportation shall be decided as occasion arises.

Article IX.—Details regarding the actual performance of this Agreement shall be discussed by mutual agreement of the delegates appointed by the Military Authorities of the two countries concerned.

Article X.—Neither of the two countries shall disclose the contents of the Agreement and its appendix, and the same shall be treated as military secrets.

Article XI.—This Agreement shall become valid when it is approved by both governments after being signed by the military representatives of the two countries. As to the proper moment for the beginning of war operations, the same shall be decided by the highest organs of the two countries. The provisions of this Agreement and the detailed steps arising therefrom shall become null and void on the day the joint war measures against the enemy end.

Article XII.—Two copies of the Chinese and of the Japanese text of this Agreement shall be drawn, one of each shall be kept by China and Japan. The Chinese and Japanese texts shall be identical in meaning.

Selected Bibliography

1. BIBLIOGRAPHIES

There are no general bibliographies covering the Orient. The following are a few of the most important on special topics and countries:

Courant, M., *Bibliographie Coréanne* (3 Vols., Paris, 1896).

Select List of Books (with references to periodicals) Relating to the Far East, and *Select List of References on Chinese Immigration,* compiled by A. P. C. Griffin, Library of Congress, Washington, 1904.

Japan Year Book, bibliography (Tokyo).

Von Wenckstern, F., *Bibliography of the Japanese Empire* (Vol. 1, Leiden, 1895; Vol. 2, Tokyo, 1907).

Bibliographies appear at the end of each country in:

The Encyclopedia Britannica (11th edition, London, 1910).

The New International Encyclopedia (2d edition, New York, 1914).

Statesman's Year Book (London).

For all books published on the subject in the British Empire consult:

British Museum Catalogues (London).

The Publishers' Circular ltd. (Fetter Lane, E. C., London).

For American publications consult:

Book Review Digest (monthly) and *Record of Cumulative Book Index* (annual), published by the H. W. Wilson Co., White Plains, N. Y.

Publishers' Trade List Annual and *The Publishers' Weekly,* published by the R. R. Bowker Co., New York City.
United States Catalogue of Books in Print (Jan. 1, 1912).
United States Library of Congress Catalogue.

II. Sources

Treaties, Documents, Government Reports, Memoirs, etc.:

Drage, Geoffrey, *Russian Affairs,* Appendix, 647–729 (London, 1904).

Hertlet, China *Treaties: Treaties, etc., between Great Britain and China, and between China and Foreign Powers,* 3d Edition, 2 Vols. (London, 1908).

McKenzie, F. A., *The Tragedy of Korea,* Appendix, 263–312 (New York, 1907).

Mannix, W. F., *Memoirs of Li Hung Chang* (New York, 1913).

Millard, Thomas F., *Our Eastern Question,* Appendix, 393–543 (New York, 1916).

Pooley, A. M., *The Secret Memoirs of Count Tadasu Hayashi* (London, 1915).

Consult also the *United States Statutes at Large, Diplomatic Correspondence, Foreign Relations, Consular and Trade Reports* (Government Printing Office, Washington).

The Bureau of Statistics has published:

Commercial China in 1904: Area, Population, Production, Railways, Telegraphs, and Transportation Routes, and Foreign Commerce and Commerce of the United States with China (Summary of Commerce and Finance, January, 1904).

Commercial Japan in 1904: Area, Population, Production, Railways, Telegraphs, and Transportation Routes, and Foreign Commerce and

Commerce of the Unitel States with Japan (Summary of Commerce and Finance, February, 1904).

Much source material will be found in the
British *Parliamentary Papers, China.*
British *Foreign Office Reports on the Trade of Korea, Annual Series.*
British *Annual Consular Reports* (London).
Chinese Imperial Customs Reports (Shanghai).
Japanese Official Publications (Tokyo):
Constitution of the Empire of Japan (1889).
Financial and Economic Annual of Japan.
Reports of the Various Government Departments (annual).
Returns of the Foreign Commerce and Trade of Japan (annual).

The Japanese Government also publishes the following books primarily for the purpose of informing the Western public:
Annual Report on Reforms and Progress in Chosen (Seoul).
Korea Year Book (Seoul).
An Official Guide to Eastern Asia: Vol. I., Manchuria and Chosen; Vols. II. and III., Japan; Vol. IV. China (Tokyo and London, 1916).

III. SECONDARY WORKS ON POLITICAL, HISTORICAL, ECONOMIC, AND DIPLOMATIC RELATIONS

A. Histories:
Boulger, Demetrius C., *The History of China,* revised edition (London, 1900).
Brinkley, Frank, *Japan and China,* 12 Vols. (London, 1903–1904).
Griffis, William Elliot, *Corea, the Hermit Nation* (New York, 1897).
"   *The Mikado's Empire,* 2 Vols. (New York, 1904).
Hosic, Alexander, *Manchuria: Its People, Resources, and History* (London, 1901).

Hulbert, H. B., *The History of Korea*, 3 Vols. (Seoul, 1905).

Longford, Joseph H., *The Story of Old Japan* (London, 1910).
"   *The Story of Korea* (New York, 1911).

Macgowan, J., *A History of China from the Earliest Days Down to the Present* (London, 1897).

McLaren, Walter W., *A Political History of Japan During the Meiji Era, 1867–1912* (New York, 1916).

Parker, Edward H., *China, Past and Present* (London, 1903).

Williams, Samuel W., *A History of China* (New York, 1897).
"   The Middle Kingdom, 2 Vols. (New York, 1883).

B. American Relations with the Far East:
Callahan, J. M., *American Relations in the Pacific and the Far East* (Baltimore, 1901).

Colquhoun, A. R., *Greater America* (New York, 1904).

Coolidge, A. C., *The United States as a World Power* (New York, 1908).

Fish, Carl Russell, *American Diplomacy* (New York, 1915).

Foster, John W., *American Diplomacy in the Orient* (New York, 1903).

Latane, J. H., *America as a World Power* (American *Nation*, XXV., New York, 1907).

C. American-Japanese Relations Including the Question of Japanese Immigration, Naturalization in America, etc.
Flowers, Montaville, *Japanese Conquest of American Opinion* (New York, 1916).

Gulick, Sidney L., *The American Japanese Problem* (New York, 1914).
" *American Democracy and Asiatic Citizenship* (New York, 1918).
Kawakami, K. K., *American Japanese Relations* (New York, 1912).
" *Asia at the Door* (New York, 1914).
Japan to America, edited by Naoichi Masaoka (Japan, 1915).
Mills, Harry Alvin, *The Japanese Problem in the United States* (New York, 1914).
Nitobe, Inazo O., *Intercourse between the United States and Japan* (Baltimore, 1891).
America to Japan, edited by Lindsay Russell (New York, 1915).
Steiner, J. F., *The Japanese Invasion* (Chicago, 1917).
Treat, Payson J., *Early Diplomatic Relations between the United States and Japan* (Baltimore, 1917).
[Books on Chinese Immigration are not listed in this bibliography. Those who desire to study the subject should consult *Select List of References on Chinese Immigration,* compiled by A. P. C. Griffin, Library of Congress, Washington, 1904.]

D. China-Japanese War:
History of Peace Negotiations between China and Japan, officially revised (Tientsin, 1895).
United States *Foreign Relations,* 1894, appendix i.
" Vladimir," *The China-Japanese War* (London, 1896).

E. Boxer War:
British *Parliamentary Papers* (1900), *China,* Nos. 3, 4.
Clements, Paul H., *The Boxer Rebellion: A*

Political and Diplomatic Review in *Columbia University Studies in History, Economics and Public Law*, Vol. 66 (New York, 1915).

Martin, W. A. P., *The Siege in Peking* (New York, 1900).

Rockhill, W. W., *Report on Affairs in China*, published in *Foreign Relations* (1901).

Thompson, H. C., *China and the Powers* (London, 1902).

F. Russo-Japanese War:

Asakawa, K., *The Russo-Japanese Conflict: Its Causes and Issues* (New York, 1904).

Hershey, Amos S., *The International Law and Diplomacy of the Russo-Japanese War* (New York, 1906).

Kuropatkin, A. M., *The Russian Army and the Japanese War* (London, 1909).

McCarthy, Michail J., *The Coming Power* (London, 1905).

Ross, C., *The Russo-Japanese War* (London, 1912).

Sedgwick, F. R., *The Russo-Japanese War* (New York, 1909).

Smith, F. E., *International Law as Interpreted during the Russo-Japanese War* (Boston, 1907).

War Department, U. S. Army, *Epitome of the Russo-Japanese War* (Washington).

G. Political and Economic Questions:

Blakeslee, G. H. (Editor), *China and the Far East* (Clark University Lectures, New York, 1910).

Brown, Arthur Judson, *The Mastery of the Far East* (New York, 1919).

Colquhoun, A. C., *The Mastery of the Pacific* (New York, 1902).

Douglas, R. K., *Europe and the Far East* (London, 1913).

Gulick, Sidney L., *The White Peril in the Far East* (New York, 1905).

Harding, Gardner L., *Present-day China* (New York, 1916).

Hornbeck, Stanley K., *Contemporary Politics in the Far East* (New York, 1916).

Hozumi, N., *The New Japanese Civil Code* (Tokyo, 1904).

Hsu, Mongton Chih, *Railway Problems in China (Columbia University Studies in History, Economics, and Public Law,* Vol. 66, New York, 1915).

Japan Year Book (Tokyo).

The Japan Directory (annual), published by *Japan Gazette* (Yokohama).

Kent, P. H., *Railway Enterprise in China* (London, 1907).

Knapp, A. M., *Feudal and Modern Japan* (Boston, 1897).

Lawton, Lancelot, *Empires of the Far East* (Boston, 1912).

Lee, Homer, *The Valor of Ignorance* (New York, 1909).

Lenox, Simpson Bertram, *Manchu and Muscovite* (New York, 1904).
"   *The True in the East and Its Aftermath* (New York, 1907).
"   *The Coming Struggle in Eastern Asia* (New York, 1908).

Little, A., *The Far East* (London, 1905).

McKenzie, F. A., *The Tragedy of Korea* (New York, 1907).
"   *The Unveiled East* (New York 1907).

Mahan, A. T., *The Problem of Asia and its Effect on International Policies* (Boston, 1900).

Martin, W. A. P., *The Awakening of China* (New York, 1907).

Millard, Thomas F., *The New Far East* (New York, 1906).

"   *America and the Far Eastern Question* (New York, 1909).

"   *Our Eastern Question* (New York, 1916).

"   *Democracy and the Eastern Question* (New York, 1919).

The New Atlas and Gazetteer of China, published by the *North-China Daily News* (Shanghai, 1917).

Norman, Henry, *The Peoples and Politics of the Far East* (New York, 1895).

Okuma, Count Shigenobu, *Fifty Years of New Japan*, English version edited by Marcus B. Huish, 2 Vols. (London, 1909).

Porter, Robert P., *Japan, the New World Power* (London, 1915).

Reinsch, Paul S., *World Politics* (New York, 1900).

"   *Intellectual and Political Currents in the Far East* (New York, 1911).

Wagel, S. R., *Chinese Currency and Banking* (Shanghai, 1915).

China Year Book, edited by H. G. W. Woodhead and H. T. Montague Bell (London).

Yen, H. L., *A Survey of Constitutional Development in China* (New York, 1911).

IV. BOOKS OF TRAVEL, DESCRIPTION, AND
        INTERPRETATION

Allen, Horace N., *Things Korean* (New York, 1908).

Ball, J. D., *Things Chinese* (Hongkong, 1903).

Birth, J. G., *Travels in North and Central China* (London, 1902).

Bishop, Isabella Bird, *Unbeaten Tracks of Japan*, 2 Vols. (fourth edition, London, 1885).
"   *Korea and Her Neighbors*, 2 Vols. (London, 1897).
"   *The Yangtze Valley and Beyond*, 2 Vols. (New York, 1900).
Chamberlain, B. H., *Things Japanese* (fifth edition, London, 1905).
Clarke, J. I. C., *Japan at First Hand* (New York, 1918).
Davidson, J. W., *The Island of Formosa* (London, 1903).
Dickinson, G. Lowes, *Letters from a Chinese Official* (New York, 1903).
"   *An Essay on the Civilization of India, China, and Japan* (London, 1914).
Fang, Wu Ting, *America Through the Spectacles of an Oriental Diplomat* (New York, 1914).
Finck, Henry T., *Lotus Time in Japan* (New York, 1898).
Griffis, W. E., *The Religions of Japan* (New York, 1895).
"   *The Mikado—Institution and Person* (Princeton University Press, 1915).
Gulick, Sidney L., *Evolution of the Japanese* (New York, 1903).
Hamilton, Angus, *Korea* (London, 1903).
Hearn, Lafcadio, *Glimpses of Unfamiliar Japan* (New York, 1894).
"   *Japan: An Attempt at Interpretation* (New York, 1904).
Hulbert, H. B., *The Passing of Korea* (New York, 1906).
Kemp, E. G., *The Face of Manchuria, Korea, and Russian Turkestan* (London, 1912).
Lowell, Percival, *Chosen: the Land of Morning Calm* (London, 1886).

Mabie, H. W., *Japan To-day and To-morrow* (New York, 1914).

Martin, W. A. P., *The Lore of Cathay* (New York, 1901).

Nitobe, I., *Bushido* (New York, 1905).

" 		*The Japanese Nation* (New York, 1912).

Ross, E. A., *The Changing Chinese* (New York, 1911).

Scherer, James A. B., *Japan To-day* (Philadelphia, 1904).

" 		*Young Japan* (Philadelphia, 1905).

Smith, Arthur H., *Village Life in China* (New York, 1899).

Starr, Frederick, *Korean Buddhism* (Boston, 1918).

V. NEWSPAPERS AND MAGAZINES DEVOTED TO FAR EASTERN AFFAIRS

A. Published in the West:

Asia: Journal of the American Asiatic Association (monthly, New York).

The Asiatic Review (formerly *The Asiatic Quarterly,* published every six weeks, London).

The Chinese Review (monthly, London).

Japan Society Bulletin (published by the Japan Society of America, New York).

Revue d'Asiatique, published by La soceité del Asiatique (monthly, Paris).

B. In China:

(1) Periodicals:

The Chinese Recorder (monthly, Shanghai).

The Chinese Social and Political Science Review (quarterly, Peking).

The Far East (monthly, Shanghai).

The Far Eastern Review (weekly, Shanghai).

Millard's Review (weekly, Shanghai).
The National Review (monthly, Shanghai).
North-China Herald (weekly, Shanghai).
(2) Dailies:
   China Press (Shanghai).
   North-China Daily News (Shanghai).
   Peking Gazette (Peking).
   Peking Daily News (Peking).
   Shanghai Gazette (Shanghai).

C. In Japan:
   (1) Periodicals:
      The Far East (weekly, Tokyo).
      The Japan Magazine (monthly, Tokyo).
      The New East (monthly, Tokyo).
      Oriental Economist (trimonthly, Tokyo).
      Tokyo Economist (weekly, Tokyo).
   (2) Dailies:
      Japan Advertiser (Tokyo).
      Japan Chronicle (formerly *Kobe Chronicle,*
      Kobe).
      Japan Gazette (Yokohama).
      Japan Mail (Tokyo).
      Japan Times (Tokyo).
      Kobe Herald (Kobe).
      Nagasaki Press (Nagasaki).

D. In Korea:
   The Korea Magazine (a monthly started by
   American missionaries in Korea, January,
   1917, devoted to ancient culture and civiliza-
   tion of Korea; published in Seoul).
   Seoul Press (an English daily subsidized by the
   Japanese Government; published in Seoul).